THE ANCIENT
NEAR EASTERN
WORLD

THE WORLD IN ANCIENT TIMES

RONALD MELLOR &
AMANDA H. PODANY
GENERAL EDITORS

THE ANCIENT NEAR EASTERN WORLD

Amanda H. Podany & Marni McGee

OXFORD
UNIVERSITY PRESS

For Emily and Nicholas —A. P.
For Mary Beth and William Sears McGee —M. M.

OXFORD
UNIVERSITY PRESS

Oxford   New York
Auckland   Bangkok   Buenos Aires   Cape Town   Chennai   Dar es Salaam   Delhi   Hong Kong   Istanbul
Karachi   Kolkata Kuala Lumpur   Madrid   Melbourne   Mexico City   Mumbai   Nairobi   São Paulo
Shanghai   Singapore   Taipei   Tokyo   Toronto

Copyright © 2005 by Oxford University Press

Published by Oxford University Press, Inc.
198 Madison Avenue, New York, New York 10016
www.oup.com

Oxford is a registered trademark of Oxford University Press

Library of Congress Cataloging-in-Publication Data

Podany, Amanda H.
   The ancient Near Eastern world / Amanda H. Podany and Marni McGee.
      p. cm. — (The world in ancient times)
   Includes bibliographical references and index.
   ISBN-13: 978-0-19-516159-5 -- 978-0-19-522245-6 (California edition) -- 978-0-19-522242-5 (set)
   ISBN-10: 0-19-516159-9 -- 0-19-522245-8 (California edition) -- 0-19-522242-3 (set)
   1. Middle East—History—To 622—Juvenile literature. 2. Middle East—Antiquities—Juvenile literature.
I. McGee, Marni. II. Title. III. Series.
   DS62.23.P63 2005
   939'.4—dc22
                                          2004013622
9 8 7 6 5 4 3 2 1

Printed in United States of America on acid-free paper

Design: Stephanie Blumenthal
Layout: Amy Henderson
Cover design and logo: Nora Wertz

On the cover: A Mesopotamian woman, seated on a stool, holds up a spindle wrapped with yarn.
Frontispiece: A priest or servant leads a bull by a nose ring to the altar as a sacrifice to the gods.

**RONALD MELLOR &
AMANDA H. PODANY**
GENERAL EDITORS

CONTENTS

A  *marks each chapter's primary sources—ancient writings and artifacts that "speak" to us from the past.*

CAST OF CHARACTERS

Because The World in Ancient Times *covers many cultures, we use the abbreviations* CE *for "Common Era" and* BCE *for "Before the Common Era." The traditional equivalents are* BC *for "Before Christ" and* AD *for "Anno Domini," Latin for "In the Year of Our Lord," referring to the birth of Jesus Christ.*

Abraham • Man described in the Hebrew Bible as the patriarch of the Israelite people

Adad-Guppi (ah-dahd-GOO-pee), 649–547 BCE • A priestess of the moon god Sin and mother of the Neo-Babylonian king Nabonidus

Adam • Man described in the Hebrew Bible as the first human being

Alexander the Great, 356–321 BCE • Macedonian king of the Greeks who conquered the Persian Empire

Amenhotep III (ah-men-HOE-tep), ruled 1387–1350 BCE • Egyptian king (also called Nimmureya) who married Princess Tadu-Heba of Syria

Ammurapi (ah-moo-RAH-pee), ruled during 12th century BCE • Last king of Ugarit, an ancient Syrian city within the Hittite Empire

Ashurnasirpal II (ah-shur-NAH-zir-pahl), ruled 883–859 BCE • Assyrian king who expanded his empire and built a great palace at Calhu

Azitawadda (ah-ZEE-tah-WAH-dah), around 9th century BCE • Levantine king whose royal inscription describes his rule

Croesus (KREE-sus), ruled 560–547 BCE • King of Lydia, known for his wealth; defeated by King Cyrus of Persia

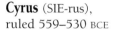

Cyrus (SIE-rus), ruled 559–530 BCE • King of the Persian Empire who conquered Babylonia in 539 BCE

Daniel, sixth century BCE • Man described in the Hebrew Bible as a holy person who survived in a den of lions

Darius I (duh-RYE-us), ruled 522–486 BCE • Persian emperor who built the city of Persepolis; introduced coins to his subjects

David, around 1000 BCE • King of Israel who united the Israelite people; made Jerusalem his capital city

Eannatum (ay-AH-nah-tum), around 2400 BCE • King of Lagash in the time of the Sumerian city-states

Enheduanna (en-HEH-doo-AH-nah), 24th century BCE • A high priestess of the moon god; first known author in history

Enkidu (EN-kee-doo) • Legendary best friend of Gilgamesh

Eve • Person described in the Hebrew Bible as the first woman

Gilgamesh (GIL-guh-mesh), around 2600 BCE • King of Uruk, whose legendary adventures are recorded in the Epic of Gilgamesh

Hammurabi
(HAHM-oo-RAH-
bee), ruled
1792–1750
BCE • King of
Babylon who
built an
empire; best
known for
his collection
of laws

Haya-Sumu (HIE-ya-SOO-moo),
18th century BCE • King who
married two daughters of Zimri-
Lim

Herodotus (huh-RAH-duh-tus),
fifth century BCE • Greek historian who described Babylon and
also the war between Persia and
Greece

Ibubu (ih-BOO-boo), around 2400
BCE • Steward of the palace at Ebla

Ilsha-hegalli (IL-sha-hay-GAHL-
lee), 17th century BCE • Mother
of Ur-Utu

Inanna-mansum (in-AHN-na-
MAN-soom), 17th century BCE •
Priest and father of Ur-Utu

Inib-sharri (IN-ib-SHAR-ree), 18th
century BCE • Daughter of King
Zimri-Lim

Isaac (EYE-zak) • Son of the
patriarch Abraham; father of the
Israelite people, according to the
Hebrew Bible

Ishmael (ISH-may-el) • Son of the
patriarch Abraham; father of the
Arab people, according to the
Hebrew Bible

Jacob • Great Israelite leader
according to the Hebrew Bible;
son of Isaac and father of many
sons, including Joseph

Jehoiachin (je-HOY-ah-keen),
ruled 598–597 BCE • Last king of
Judah; taken captive by the Neo-
Babylonians

Joseph • Favorite son of Jacob
according to the Hebrew Bible;
became powerful in Egypt

Josiah (jo-SIE-ya), ruled 639–609
BCE • King of Judah who
reformed the religious practices
of the Israelites

Kirum (KEY-room), 18th century
BCE • Daughter of Zimri-Lim of
Mari and wife of Haya-Sumu

Mebaragesi (may-BAH-rah-GAY-
see), around 2700 BCE • King of
Umma in the time of Sumerian
city-states; author of the earliest
known royal inscription.
Sometimes called En-mebaragesi,
or Lord Mebaragesi

Moses • Leader of the Israelites,
said in the Hebrew Bible to have
led them out of slavery and
received the Ten Commandments
from Yahweh

Mursili (MUHR-see-lee), ruled
around 1620–1590 BCE • Hittite
king who raided the city of
Babylon in 1595; brought an end
to Hammurabi's empire

Nabonidus (nah-boh-NIE-dus),
ruled 555–539 BCE • Last king of
the Neo-Babylonian Empire;
devoted to the moon god Sin

Naomi (nay-OH-mee) • Israelite
described in the Hebrew Bible as
mother-in-law of Ruth and great-
great-grandmother of King David

Naram-Sin (NAH-rahm-SIN),
ruled 2260–2223 BCE • King of
the Akkadian Empire and grandson of Sargon; presented himself
as divine

Nebuchadnezzar II (NEB-yoo-
kad-NEZ-er), ruled 605–562 BCE
• Neo-Babylonian king who
enlarged the empire; conquered
Judah

Ningallam (nin-GAH-lahm), 24th
century BCE • Slave woman who
raised pigs for the queen's household at Lagash during the time
of the Sumerian city-states

Ninshubur-tayar (nin-SHOO-
bur-TIE-yar), 18th century BCE •
Farmer who adopted a son
named Patiya in the reign of
Samsu-iluna

Noah • Man described in the
Hebrew Bible as the good man
who survived a great flood

Omri (OHM-ree), ruled 885–874
BCE • King of Israel who sent
tribute to Assyria

Pagirum (PAH-gee-rum), 17th century BCE • Scribe who lived in
Terqa and was given a land grant
by the local king

Patiya (pa-TEE-ya), 18th century
BCE • Young Mesopotamian man
adopted by Ninshubur-tayar in
the reign of Samsu-iluna

Puabi (poo-AH-bee), around 2500 BCE • Sumerian queen whose burial was the richest of the royal tombs of Ur

Ra'imtum (Ra-IM-tum), 17th century BCE • Wife of Ur-Utu

Ruth (rooth) • Moabite described in the Hebrew Bible as Naomi's daughter-in-law and great-grandmother of King David

Samsu-ditana (SAM-soo-dee-TAH-nah), ruled 1625–1595 BCE • Last king of the Old Babylonian Empire; ruler when Hittites raided Babylon

Samsu-iluna (SAM-soo-ih-LOO-nah), ruled 1749–1712 BCE • Son of Hammurabi; king of the Old Babylonian Empire who lost control of the southern part of the empire

Samuel, 11th century BCE • Religious leader, described in the Hebrew Bible as having anointed the first two kings of Israel, Saul and David

Sargon (SAR-gon), ruled 2340–2284 BCE • King of Akkad who built the world's first empire; subject of many legends

Saul, 11th century BCE • First king of Israel who often fought against the Philistines, according to the Hebrew Bible

Sennacherib (sen-NAH-keh-rib), ruled 704–681 BCE • Assyrian king who destroyed Babylon

Shamash-nasir (SHAH-mahsh-NAHT-seer), 18th or 17th century BCE • Adopted son who went to court to claim his inheritance

Shibtu (SHIB-too), 18th century BCE • Queen of Mari, wife of Zimri-Lim, many of whose letters have survived

Shimatum (SHIH-mah-toom), 18th century BCE • Daughter of Zimri-Lim of Mari and wife of Haya-Sumu

Shulgi (SHOOL-gee), ruled 2094–2047 BCE • King of the Third Dynasty of Ur; author of the first collection of laws

Sin-leqe-unnini (SIN LAY-kay oo-NEE-nee), around 12th century BCE • Scribe who wrote the Epic of Gilgamesh, based on earlier written and oral tales

Solomon (SOLL-uh-mun), 10th century BCE • ruler of Israel who, according to the Hebrew Bible, built a temple to Yahweh in Jerusalem; son of King David

Tadu-Heba (TAH-doo-HAY-bah), 14th century BCE • Princess of Mittani, who married King Amenhotep III of Egypt; daughter of Tushratta

Tira-il (TEE-rah-eel), around 2400 BCE • Scribe at Ebla whose letter is the earliest known example of diplomacy

Tushratta (toosh-RAH-tah), 14th century BCE • King of Mittani, who corresponded with fellow "great kings"; father of Tadu-Heba

Ur-Nammu (ur-NAH-moo), ruled 2113–2096 BCE • King of the Third Dynasty of Ur who supervised the building of ziggurats

Ur-Utu (ur-OO-too), 17th century BCE • Wealthy Mesopotamian priest who kept an archive of his family business

Ut-napishtim (oot-nah-PISH-tim) • Legendary Mesopotamian believed to have survived a great flood by constructing a boat

Xerxes (ZURK-seez), ruled 486–465 BCE • King of the Persian Empire, son of Darius I; tried but failed to conquer Greece

Zimri-Lim (ZIM-ree-LIM), ruled around 1775–1761 BCE • King of Mari; texts found in his palace reveal many details of palace life

Zoroaster (ZOR-oh-ASS-ter), early first millennium BCE • Religious teacher in Persia who founded Zoroastrianism

THE ANCIENT NEAR EASTERN WORLD

EUROPE

GREECE

Black Sea

Caspian Sea

Lydia

•Hattusa

ANATOLIA
(TURKEY)

MESOPOTAMIA
(IRAQ)

Lukka

Hatti

Taurus Mountains

Tigris River

•Carchemish   Harran•

•Nineveh

Mediterranean Sea

Ebla•   •Aleppo

Mittani   Assyria

Alashiya
(Cyprus)   Ugarit•

Umm el-Marra   •Calhu

SYRIA

•Ashur

Bisitun•

Phoenicia

Euphrates River

Terqa•

LEVANT   Mari•

Zagros Mountains

Canaan

Israel

Agade•   •Sippar

Akkad   •Kish   Babylonia

•Jerusalem   Babylon•   •Nippur

Elam

Judah   Moab

Umma•   •Lagash

Nile River

Uruk•   •Ur

Media

Sumer   •Eridu

•Persepolis

•Amarna

EGYPT

Dilmun
(Bahrain)   Persian Gulf

Thebes

Red Sea

ARABIA

AFRICA

ASIA

Aral Sea

Oxus River

PERSIA
(IRAN)

Indus River

Meluhha

[M]agan
([O]man)

Arabian Sea

| 0 | | 400 mi |
| 0 | | 600 km |

SOME PRONUNCIATIONS

Agade (uh-GAHD-ay)
Akkad (AHK-ahd)
Alashiya (ahl-ah-SHEE-uh)
Ashur (ASH-er)
Assyria (uh-SEER-ee-uh)
Babylon (BAB-uh-lon)
Babylonia (bab-uh-LO-nee-uh)
Calhu (CAL-hoo)
Canaan (KAY-nun)
Carchemish (KAR-kuh-mish)
Ebla (EB-luh)
Eridu (EHR-uh-doo)
Euphrates River (YOO-fray-teez)
Harran (huh-RAHN)
Hatti (HAH-tee)
Hattusa (hah-TOO-sah)
Lagash (LAH-gahsh)
Levant (luh-VANT)
Mari (MAR-ee)
Mesopotamia (MES-uh-puh-TAY-mee-uh)
Mittani (mih-TAH-nee)
Nineveh (NIN-uh-vuh)
Nippur (NIP-ur)
Persepolis (per-SEP-uh-lus)
Persia (PER-zhuh)
Phoenicia (fi-NISH-uh)
Sumer (SOO-mehr)
Syria (SEER-ee-uh)
Terqa (TAIR-kuh)
Tigris River (TIE-griss)
Ugarit (oo-GAH-rit)
Umm el-Marra (OOM-el-MAR-uh)
Ur (oor)
Uruk (UR-uhk)

The area that historians call the Near East is called the Middle East in modern times. The ancient and modern borders are not exactly the same, but the region once known as Mesopotamia is now called Iraq; ancient Anatolia is modern Turkey; the Levant is now Israel, Jordan, Lebanon, and the Palestinian territories; and Persia's new name is Iran. Only Syria has kept its ancient name.

INTRODUCTION
THE SHAPE OF THINGS TO COME

Can't everyone—even small children—name the country where she or he lives? Today, the answer would surely be yes, but that hasn't always been true. In ancient times, borders shifted, so that even many grown-ups had only fuzzy ideas about which land they lived in.

Ancient Mesopotamia, which was located in the region of modern Iraq, had no ancient name. The people who lived there never spoke of the whole land as we now know it. The ancient Greeks later came up with the name Mesopotamia for the land between the Tigris and Euphrates Rivers (meso + potamia = "between" + "the rivers," in ancient Greek.)

People who lived in Mesopotamia thousands of years ago thought of themselves as belonging to a particular city or region, where a particular language was spoken. Later, around the 15th century BCE, they began to identify themselves with the huge cities that dominated the land. At this point, historians call the flat river valley of southern Mesopotamia "Babylonia," and the hills of northern Mesopotamia "Assyria."

Historians have tried to figure out exactly where the borders of the ancient lands were, but it's often hard to do. So they sometimes look at wider areas where the people shared a common culture. The ancient Near East is just such a region. The lands of Mesopotamia (modern Iraq), Anatolia (modern Turkey), Persia (modern Iran), the Levant (modern Jordan, Lebanon, Israel, and the Palestinian territories), and Syria shared many things in ancient times—perhaps most important was their writing system. We could call them the "cuneiform lands," the places where educated people used a wedge-shaped writing system to inscribe their words and ideas on clay tablets.

The cuneiform writing system developed in Mesopo-

MAPLES FOR REMEMBERING

The first letters of the Near Eastern regions spell MAPLES: Mesopotamia, Anatolia, Persia, the Levant, Egypt, and Syria. Even though Egypt was part of this ancient world, scholars study it separately because it had a different writing system and different religious beliefs from the rest of the Near East.

tamia, but over time it spread to neighboring lands. Along with the writing system came trade, a shared interest in law and literature, and a similar way of thinking about the gods. The cuneiform sign for the storm god's name, for example, was the same in many lands, including Mesopotamia and Syria. People from Mesopotamia would read that sign as "Adad." But in Canaan, where the storm god had a different name, people would read it as "Baal."

The history of the cuneiform lands starts with the first cities, around 3500 BCE, and lasts for more than 3,000 years. Historians and archaeologists piece together the history of the cuneiform lands by studying the stories of commoners and kings, warriors and lawmakers, inventors and adventurers, scribes and priestesses, and by carefully examining the objects and buildings they left behind.

WHY IS 1700 IN THE 18TH CENTURY?

The 18th century BCE—during the height of the ancient Near Eastern civilization—took place in the 1700s BCE. It may seem that this century ought to be the 17th, because the year numbers all begin with 17—1706, 1707, 1708, and so on. But it isn't, because the 100s were actually the *second* century.

Although most cuneiform tablets were rectangular, many were barrel-shaped, like this one. Students wrote on circular tablets, and royal scribes sometimes used prism-shaped tablets for their royal inscriptions.

CHAPTER 1

ANCIENT TRASH AND BURIED TREASURE
ARCHAEOLOGISTS AT WORK

Syria's steep cliffs drop right to the edge of the Euphrates River, creating a narrow valley. But in the distance, green fields flourish, made rich by water from the river.

It's early morning. The sun hasn't risen, but the sky has begun to turn pink in the east. The Euphrates River looks like a silver streak against the black landscape. Roosters crow in the small village of Tell Ashara in the Middle Eastern country of Syria. Voices call to one another in Arabic as farmers walk along the dusty roads to their fields. In one of the mud-brick houses, men and women sit around a wooden table, sharing a breakfast of pita bread, yogurt, hard-boiled eggs, and oranges, washed down with cups of instant coffee. They're planning their day's work, deciding where to dig. They speak in English, Italian, Arabic, and French.

Who are these people, and what are they up to? They are archaeologists, and their work combines the talents of historians, junk collectors, scientists, and detectives. They are paid to be nosy, exploring the buried secrets of people who lived hundreds or thousands of years ago by digging up ancient cities and towns. Why are they up so early? To keep from melting! By afternoon, the mercury could hit a sizzling 115 degrees Fahrenheit or more in the shade. So the archaeologists at Tell Ashara do most of their work early in the day.

The archaeologists walk from their house to the *tell*—a huge hill rising from the plain. Tells (sometimes spelled *tels*) mark the places where human beings have lived, worked, and worshiped. They are made up of windblown dirt, discarded pottery, leftover bits from ancient meals, and parts of broken walls. Sometimes a town or village rests on top of the ancient remains. But often, the site has been abandoned. The word *tell* is the same in modern Arabic and Hebrew, and in the ancient languages of the Near East because these languages are all related to one another. And it works in English, too, because a tell does exactly that: it *tells* about the past. It's an archaeologist's workshop.

The archaeologists at Tell Ashara—like the archaeologists at dozens of places in the Near East—carry picks, notebooks, digging tools, laptop computers, and bag lunches to the work site. Flat fields line the path to the tell on both sides. Manmade ditches between the fields carry water to the thirsty crops that grow there, mostly wheat and barley. Poplar trees mark the boundaries between fields. Orchards of palms and apricot trees patch the landscape with green and gold.

Workmen from the nearby village join the archaeologists at the tell. These men wear headscarves for protection from the burning sun. They have walked to work or ridden on bicycles, motorcycles, or even donkeys. Many of these workers have been excavating local sites for years, and they know how to "read" what they see in the ground.

Together, the archaeologists and workmen at Tell Ashara gradually uncover the remains of an ancient city where people lived for thousands of years. In ancient times, it was called Terqa, and it was one of the biggest cities in ancient Syria. As with all archaeological sites, the most recent remains are in the top levels. In the mud at the top, the archaeologists found ballpoint pens and blue jeans from only a few years ago. The oldest remains lie at the bottom, and are more than five thousand years old.

Thousands of tells dot the landscape in the Near East, so how do archaeologists decide where to dig? They usually lean toward larger tells. And they tend to avoid tells that are partly covered by modern buildings. But there are usually many tells to choose from, so the archaeologists collect

A deep trench cuts through the tell at Jericho, revealing recent materials at the top and very ancient remains below. People lived in Jericho even before the invention of pottery, thousands of years ago.

HOW BIG IS BIG?

More than 12 million people live in Tokyo today and 8 million inhabit New York City. A big city in the ancient world seems tiny by comparison. A thriving Mesopotamian city might have only ten thousand inhabitants, but that was huge, compared to a village.

pottery sherds—broken pieces—from the surface of each tell. They try to imagine what the pot looked like when it was new. Was it tall and thin, or was it short and thick? Was its surface rough or shiny? Did the potter paint his pot or leave it plain? Because pottery styles were different at different times, the answers to these questions help archaeologists figure out when the pot would have been used and, from that information, when the tell was occupied. When their choice is final, the team begins to work.

To most people, a dig looks like a big hole in the ground. Everything is the same pale brown color—all made of mud and clay. But a trained eye can pick out pieces of a wall, part of a floor, or even a few baked tiles. The workmen carry dirt out of the pit in buckets. The archaeologists help with the digging, using trowels, picks, and brushes. And everyone watches for scorpions because of their poisonous stings.

The archaeologists all have special jobs to do. Some direct the local workmen. Others write down exactly where each "find" was discovered. The "findspot" helps to pinpoint how each object was used and when it was buried or thrown away. For example, a room with many pots that contain the remains of food was probably a pantry. And a pantry on the lowest level of the tell will be much older than one higher up. One archaeologist takes hundreds of

A modern village rests atop an ancient tell, formed by the remains of a town that was buried long ago. For thousands of years, people used the water from the nearby Euphrates River to water their crops.

photos and describes each discovery in a notebook. Another specializes in plant remains. Yet another is a pottery expert. One of the archaeologists records all the written documents that are uncovered, if there are any, and later translates them. A specialist in animal bones identifies different animals from the remains of their bones. A **conservator** helps to protect everything that is found. All these people have the same goal: to learn as much as they can about the ancient village or city and its people by studying what they discover in the ground.

Conservators try to protect ancient objects, sometimes treating them with special materials to keep them from falling apart. Sunlight and moisture in the air can damage or destroy these treasures.

What archaeologists usually find isn't very glamorous. We call it "buried treasure" because of the story it tells. In fact, it's mostly trash that nobody wanted anymore: broken pottery and bricks, bone scraps left after a meal, or a cracked grinding stone that women once used to make flour for baking. Almost everything that has survived is made of bone, stone, or clay. Archaeologists almost never find straw mats, carpets, clothes, or baskets. These materials will have fallen apart long ago. Harder materials such as copper and bronze aren't found very often either because people tended to re-use them instead of throwing them away. Often valuable things were buried in the tombs of kings, queens, and other wealthy people, but grave robbers have stolen most of these treasures—though not all of them.

Glenn Schwartz, a university professor and archaeologist, got lucky. He and his students were working at a dig site called Umm el-Marra, in Syria. They were astonished to discover a tomb that the thieves had missed. Inside, they found both human and animal remains. Among the dry, white bones were gold and silver treasures. Very few archaeologists have the thrill of discovering a tomb like that one. But they can learn a lot from ordinary tells—from what people left or threw away.

What if someone was trying to understand *your* family by going through your trash? What artifacts would they find? A used-up watercolor set, a magazine with a page torn out, or a tomato-stained pizza box? (Any bits of pepperoni

Continues on page 22

Gold headband
from Umm
el-Marra, Syria, 2300 BCE

ARCHAEOLOGIST AT WORK: AN INTERVIEW WITH GLENN SCHWARTZ

Glenn Schwartz *takes notes on a tomb, while student Alice Petty cleans a bone using a dental tool. Dr. Schwartz wears a headscarf for protection against the broiling sun. He is a professor of Near Eastern studies in the Krieger School of Arts and Sciences at Johns Hopkins University in Baltimore, Maryland. He is the leader of a team of archaeologists and graduate students working on a tell at Umm el-Marra, believed to be the site of Tuba, one of first cities of ancient Syria. Graduate students, like Petty, have already been to college. They go back to a university to work on their favorite subject—archaeology or history, for example. After years of study, they may become professional archaeologists, conservators, historians, or professors themselves.*

How did you discover the tomb at Umm el-Marra?

My graduate students and I had been investigating this tell since 1994. In the fall of 2000, we were digging at the highest point of the tell, which would have been the center of the ancient city. Because temples were built on high mud-brick platforms in the center of the city, we dug at the tell's highest point, hoping to discover a buried palace or temple. We were very disappointed to find that there wasn't one. Instead, we found a really big heap of stones. We didn't know what to make of this mound. Sometimes, in archaeology, you find things that just don't make any sense. I told Alice Petty, one of my graduate students, to make sure that all of the stones were sketched and photographed and then to get rid of them. So she did that and immediately hit on what seemed to be a small, rectangular room with stone walls.

Were you excited to discover a buried room?

Not really. That wasn't too exciting, especially when you're hoping for a palace. But then we realized that the room was full of unbroken pottery. Now *that* was unusual. Most things are in bits and pieces by the time we find them, thousands of years after they've been used and thrown out.

Up to that point, Alice hadn't been particularly lucky with her finds. She never seemed to find anything really wonderful. In fact, a couple of nights before, at dinner when we had chicken, she was sharing a wishbone with another graduate student. She wished that she'd find something—*anything*—exciting, for once. And she won the "pull."

Sounds like her wish was coming true.
It sure was. Next she spotted some pieces of gray metal sticking up from the ground. Now, if they'd been green, we'd have known they were copper, because copper turns green as it ages. But gray meant that they were silver, which is very valuable. They looked like spearheads. But then came the big discovery. Bones! We called over the bone expert on our team, and she told us that the bones were not animals, but humans. That's how we knew it was a tomb.

Could you tell anything about these bones, other than that they had belonged to a person?
We didn't just find a few bones. We found a whole skeleton. Four skeletons, in fact. There were two young women, buried side-by-side, each with a baby beside her. Alice had found an untouched tomb. She was completely flabbergasted. It was a shock—a wonderful shock.

Who were these people—or, rather, who had they been?
We don't know for sure. But the women were buried with lots of gold, silver, and lapis lazuli—a valuable blue stone that

would have come from faraway Afghanistan. One of the babies had on a bronze collar, and one of the women had a small iron object on her necklace. Iron was unusual and valuable in those days. All this told us that the women were very wealthy, probably members of a royal family.

What else did you find in the tomb?
We noticed the top of another skull, and when we excavated further, we found a whole other layer. On this second level down were the skeletons of two men. With them was a bronze dagger and a bronze spearhead. The men had fewer valuables buried with them, as compared to the women. But one man wore a silver headband. We kept digging, of course, and found a third layer and another skeleton, another grown person buried with a small silver cup and some silver pins—kind of like ancient safety pins.

Why would so many people be buried together like that?
We can't be sure at this point, but we've got some ideas. Here's one possibility: two women and their babies died, sometime around 2300 BCE, perhaps in an epidemic... some terrible disease. We know from Mesopotamian texts that people living at this time believed in life after death. They thought you had to take gifts to give to the spirits who guarded the underworld. Otherwise, they'd give you a hard time. And because the women were royals, lower-ranking men were killed and buried with them—perhaps to serve them in the afterlife. That would explain the silver cups and valuable objects in the tomb.

Archaeologists found the skulls of two donkeys on top of a box containing the donkeys' bodies at Umm el-Marra, Syria.

What was the weirdest thing that you found in the tomb?
The weirdest thing might be donkeys. We found the skeletons of two small donkeys in a brick box next to the tomb. These creatures had been buried standing up. And their heads had been cut off. The skulls were stuck on top of the box. Then two years later, in 2002, we found more donkeys and more skulls near the tomb.

Why wasn't this tomb robbed?
I don't know. We found another tomb not far away, and it had been stripped of all its valuables. Maybe this one was honored and protected for a long time, but then maybe the roof caved in, and it was forgotten somehow. It's a puzzle. There are very few tombs found in the ancient Near East with gold and silver still in them. I guess we just got lucky!

Continued from page 19
in the corner?) Would they find a dog food can or a bag of kitty litter? Disposable diapers? Contact lens solution? Nosy snoops would learn a lot. They'd have a pretty good idea about how many people live in your home, their ages, and what each person likes. Archaeologists learn the same sorts of things from ancient trash, even though there was much less to throw away in those days.

Standing on the floor of an ancient house, surrounded by things left behind, an archaeologist may feel like a time traveler. The oven in the middle of a courtyard conjures up the image of the woman who once baked bread there. Small figures, clay wagons, and other toys bring to life the children who played, not far from their mother's watchful eye. The remains of the nearby well invite us to imagine the man of the house drawing water for his family. Wouldn't those ancient people be amazed to learn that we think about them now, thousands of years after their deaths?

CHAPTER 2

RIVERS AND DITCHES, TEMPLES AND FARMS

IRRIGATION AND THE GROWTH OF TOWNS

66 "THE LAMENTATION OVER THE DESTRUCTION OF SUMER AND AKKAD" AND A MESOPOTAMIAN TOWN

Ever since the British reporter Jonathan Glancy was young, he wanted to visit the ancient Mesopotamian town of Eridu, built almost seven thousand years ago. The exhibits in the British Museum in London had fascinated him. In an article in a British newspaper, the *Guardian*, Glancy recalled wandering through the museum's "echoing gray halls, . . . captivated by the treasures of Mesopotamia, . . . winged bulls with the heads of fierce bearded men, . . . cuneiform scripts baked . . . into brick tablets, and a jigsaw of civilizations."

66 Town of Eridu, Iraq, around 5000–4000 BCE

In 2002, Glancy's wish came true. He went to Mesopotamia, now called Iraq. When he reached Eridu, in southern Iraq, he was amazed by how dry and isolated everything seemed in the blistering hot desert. He found that, "what hits first is not history but a wall of heat and an even hotter wind. Our feet crunch across seashells— thousands of years old." Seashells in the desert? The ancient Mesopotamians

It's hard to imagine that the bleak, desert landscape at Eridu used to be a green marsh.

["] "The Lamentation over the Destruction of Sumer and Akkad," Iraq, around 2000 BCE

described Eridu as a place where river water mixed with the salty water of the sea. According to one ancient writer from around 2000 BCE, Eridu was a place "overflowing with great waters."

Eridu was once a thriving town in what the ancient Greeks called Mesopotamia, which means "land between the rivers." In fact, very few people actually lived *between* Mesopotamia's two rivers, the Tigris and the Euphrates. The climate was (and is) so hot and dry, people had to live right on the riverbanks in order to have enough water.

Archaeologists tell us that Eridu was on the bank of the Euphrates in ancient times. So why is it in the desert today, miles from water? The rivers themselves know the answer. Thousands of years ago, as the Tigris and Euphrates flowed south, they carried soil and dropped it downstream. Gradually, the build-up of fine soil and sand created a broad, flat valley between the rivers. The southern stretch of this valley has no rocks in it—nothing hard enough to make a solid bed for the rivers to flow through. So after the rivers flooded, which they did every year, they didn't always go back to the same path.

Ancient people built canals and levees—raised banks—to keep the rivers flowing near their settlements. For thousands of years, their efforts succeeded. But eventually, the rivers rebelled. Like a horse that throws off its saddle and reins, the Euphrates changed its course and left Eridu stranded in the middle of the Iraqi desert.

Even when the river flowed by Eridu, it must have been a pretty uncomfortable place to live—incredibly hot in the

summer and dry all year round. In fact, archaeologists have discovered that ancient peoples first settled in northern Mesopotamia, where it was cooler. Living among its hills, shady trees, and lush grasses, they survived by hunting wild animals for food. They gathered fruits, seeds, and roots and harvested the wheat and barley that grew wild there. Later, the villagers began to farm and to keep animals in herds. Gradually some farmers moved south into the river valley, taking their now-**domesticated** crops and animals with them.

No one knows for sure why some of these ancient peoples moved to southern Mesopotamia. Perhaps they wanted to live near the coast of the Persian Gulf, which, like the Euphrates, was closer to Eridu in those days. Perhaps they wanted to fish in the gulf and hunt wild birds on its shores. Archaeologists know, though, that by around 5000 BCE, settlers had reached the place that was later called Eridu.

Goats, sheep, and cattle all ran wild, until people learned they could fence a pair of animals and start a herd. These domesticated animals provided a regular supply of milk, meat, and wool.

The first settlers lived in reed and mud huts built on a dry sand dune, surrounded by marshes. The people grew crops in the damp soil near the marshland and fished in its waters. But then the marshes began to dry out, so the people of Eridu dug canals. At first, they dug simple ditches to bring water from the river to their fields. Over time, their irrigation system became more complex, with larger and larger canals.

The people who lived in Eridu between 5000 and 4000 BCE used the reeds that grew along the riverbanks to make baskets and mats. They also used reeds for roofing. Bones found in the tells show that dinner included fish from the river and animals, such as birds and gazelles, that lived on its banks.

The building carved in the middle of this alabaster trough was probably made from reeds. This ancient building technique is still used today in southern Iraq.

Water, reeds, and palm trees once marked the landscape in southern Mesopotamia. In ancient times, the area around Eridu would have looked like this, but now it is a desert.

The only trees that grew well in the south were palm trees. Even though their fruit, the date, was good to eat, the trees weren't very useful for building, because the wood is spongy and isn't strong enough. And because stones were scarce, the people built their homes from what the earth provided: mud and clay. In fact, the ancient people of Eridu used mud and clay for almost everything: tools, pots, and dishes. They made balls from clay and used them as ammunition in their slingshots. They even made clay sickles for cutting grain.

Archaeologists have found some things at Eridu that didn't come from southern Mesopotamia: shells and colored stones that were used for beads; hoes made of flint, a very hard stone; and knives made of obsidian. The flint was from northern Mesopotamia, and the obsidian, a glass-like rock formed in volcanoes, came from hundreds of miles away in what is now called Turkey. These objects must have come through trade. And most likely, each of them passed through many hands—ancient middlemen—before they reached Eridu.

Southern Mesopotamia was the center of the action: one of the first places in the world where villages grew into towns. Archaeologists aren't sure why this happened, but they have some ideas about it. Perhaps, as families had more children and the population grew, the **irrigation** ditches had to stretch further and be dug deeper to provide water for more land and more people. Then, as the canal system expanded, the fields became richer and the supply of food grew. Once it was irrigated, the soil of southern Mesopotamia produced even richer crops than the rain-fed fields of the north. Perhaps the good farming conditions encouraged people to settle near thriving southern towns, such as Eridu.

Traders—bringing such luxuries as flint, obsidian, and shell—flocked to the towns to find buyers for their goods. This, too, helped the towns to grow. People wanted to live in interesting places where they could find and buy exciting new things. What fun to have something *not* made out of clay!

Many early towns were built around shrines or small temples to the gods. One of Eridu's first mud-brick buildings was a shrine built around 5000 BCE and dedicated to Ea, the god of fresh water. In fact, the people of Eridu built 18 shrines and temples on that same spot over a two-thousand-year period from 5000 to 3000 BCE. Because people believed that their gods watched over them, perhaps it made them feel safer to live close to the place where their gods were kept. Any or all of these factors might have encouraged villages to grow into towns of maybe two thou-

Farmers who can't depend on rainfall to water their crops use irrigation instead. When you see sprinklers watering a field, or when you water your own lawn, you're seeing the descendants of an ancient technique the Mesopotamians invented.

Each year, the rivers laid down fine soil, called silt, that gradually raised the height of the riverbed. The river was actually higher than the land around it, as this archaeologist's drawing shows. But the water didn't spill over (except during the flood season) because the riverbanks also became higher each year. Farmers irrigated their crops by cutting a slice in the bank and letting water flow through a canal into their fields. When they had enough water for their crops, they would close up the gap.

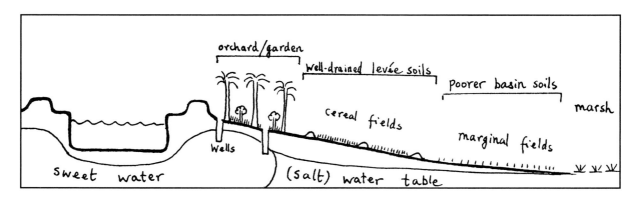

REINING IN THE RIVERS

Big canals fed smaller and even smaller canals, with the water always flowing downhill from the river. But the canals needed constant attention. Without care, they could become clogged with silt, and the water would no longer flow to the fields. The whole community worked together to dig out the extra silt so that the rivers would continue to flow beside their communities and water their fields.

sand people, and later into cities of many thousands.

No one knows who ruled over the people of Eridu at the beginning of its history. That's one of many mysteries. Archaeologists have found no palaces in the lowest (earliest) levels of the tell. This means that the people didn't have kings for thousands of years. But it's likely that someone, or maybe a special group, was in charge. Perhaps the priests who tended the statue of the local god led the population in other ways, too. Perhaps they organized the men of the town so that together they could clear out the canals, build the temples to the gods, and keep the town safe. Because people hadn't invented writing yet, we have to depend upon the tells to whisper Mesopotamia's earliest secrets.

The people who lived in Mesopotamia's ancient villages and towns were like us in many ways. Their bodies and minds were the same as ours. They could think and reason, just as we do today. They just didn't have all our equipment and know-how or some of our ideas. But new ideas were blossoming all the time.

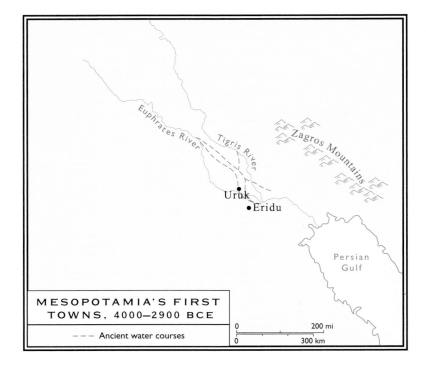

MESOPOTAMIA'S FIRST TOWNS, 4000–2900 BCE

– – – Ancient water courses

0   200 mi
0   300 km

CHAPTER 3

OF POTTERS AND POTS, PLOWMEN AND PLOWS

TECHNOLOGY AND THE FIRST CITIES

In ancient times, pots had hundreds of uses. Mesopotamians used them for storing grain, carrying water, shipping fruit (mostly dates), and cooking a stew over the fire for dinner. People drank from pottery cups and ate from pottery bowls. Sometimes they even buried their dead in pots. Archaeologists discovered these two clay pots:

A potter crafted one of them in 4500 BCE. The other was made a thousand years later, around 3500 BCE. Can you guess which is which?

Surprisingly, the painted one with the smoother surface (we'll call it Pot A) was made before the plainer one (Pot B). But why would the older pot be fancier and more carefully made than the later one? The person who made Pot A probably learned how to make pots from his father, who learned from *his* father, and so on. Potter A made pots completely by hand. First, he rolled the clay into thin ropes that he coiled into the shape he wanted. Then, using his fingers,

❝ Pots from Iraq, around 4500 *(left)* and 3500 BCE

Modern potter's wheels are very similar to those the Mesopotamians invented. Some are powered by electricity, but many potters still turn their wheels with their feet.

he made the bumpy sides thin and smooth. Afterward he painted the pot with detailed patterns and baked it in a hot kiln. The finished product was beautiful, but making it took a long time.

Then someone invented a new technology—a different way to make pots, using the **potter's wheel**. With this new method, a craftsman could spin a lump of clay on a flat wheel, which he probably turned with his feet. As the clay spun around, the potter could gather the lump between his palms, press with his thumbs to make a bowl, and then use his fingers to shape it. An expert could make many more pots than before in the same amount of time. Perhaps when it became possible to make pots so quickly, potters stopped spending so much time making them beautiful.

We can never name the inventor of the potter's wheel. We'll never know exactly when or where the invention happened either. Writing hadn't been invented yet, so we have no records.

The earliest potter's wheels were almost certainly made from wood. Because wood disintegrates in the soil, no wooden wheels have survived. We know that the potter's wheel was invented around 3500 BCE because the pots themselves tell us through tell-tale markings that appear on some pots, but not others. When a pot is spinning on the wheel, the potter's fingers trace a pattern that isn't found on coiled pots. A potter leaves a second clue when he slides a thin string under the finished pot to cut it from the still-spinning wheel. The string leaves a line on the clay. Archaeologists have found Mesopotamian pots made as early as 3500 BCE with markings that show that they were created on a wheel. This proves that potters had begun

A potter would have turned this clay wheel with his feet, leaving his hands free to shape the pot as the wheel spun.

to use wheels by 3500. Chemical tests also give information about when a pot was made. Scientists can figure out the age of the pot itself or any remains of food found inside it.

Even the gods had to farm in ancient Mesopotamia. The god behind holds the plow, while the one in front drives a team (a lion and a dragon!) with his left hand.

The potter who used a wheel probably didn't need to spend much time farming. Many of his customers would have been farmers, so he could sell or trade his pots for food. The farmers, too, had a new technology that made their lives easier: the plow, a tool for cutting, breaking up, and turning the soil to prepare it for planting. Improved farming methods meant that farmers could grow enough food not only for their own families, but also to sell or trade with others.

Archaeologists believe that the plow was invented around the same time as the potter's wheel—between 3800 and 3100 BCE. But because early plows also must have been made of wood, none have survived. Before plows were invented, farmers used ordinary sticks to break up the soil. The first plows were just pieces of sharpened wood attached to a wooden frame, which oxen dragged through a field. But wooden plows broke easily in Mesopotamia's hard, clay soil. Farmers needed something stronger. Copper worked well for earrings and bracelets but was too soft for plows.

The big break came when someone melted copper and tin together and created a brand-new metal: bronze. Was this someone's brilliant idea or an accident? Bronze objects found in tombs and temples from this period show that wealthy people used this strong, gleaming metal not only for plows, but also for bowls, pitchers, spearheads, daggers, and statues of their gods. Wealthy Mesopotamians developed a taste for the beautiful and useful things that skillful artists made from bronze—and silver, too, which was even more expensive.

There was no copper, tin, or silver to be found in Mesopotamia, so the Mesopotamians needed something to trade

Historians and archaeologists study the days, years, and centuries that have passed, exploring even the events that happened thousands and thousands of years ago. They call each one-thousand-year block a millennium.

" List, Iraq, 18th century BCE

with the people who lived where these metals could be mined. Pretty much all they had in their river valleys was mud and clay and what grew or grazed on it. But foreign traders weren't interested in trading semiprecious stones and fancy metals for pottery, which is, after all, nothing but baked clay. So what could the Mesopotamians offer? They needed to be creative—and they were.

By the fourth **millennium** (the 3000s) BCE, Mesopotamian spinners and weavers were producing beautiful cloth made from the wool of their many sheep. They traded their cloth for other luxury goods. None of these ancient fabrics survive because, like wood, cloth disintegrates in the soil. But we know that cloth was the Mesopotamians' main export for centuries because, once writing was invented, lots of documents tell us about its production. An 18th-century BCE list recorded 384 workdays spent in the creation of "one fine [wool]...robe." It must have been richly designed and embroidered.

Most spinners and weavers were women. Like potters and metalworkers, they became professionals—people who specialize in a certain kind of work, perhaps trading with others for goods or services. Mesopotamian professionals no longer did everything for themselves. Instead, some people did nothing but make pots, while others made cloth or became traders.

Trade depends on transportation. The earliest Mesopotamian traders used donkeys to carry their goods. They also used boats. And once again, an unknown inventor changed the world. This person had probably seen a potter's wheel. Perhaps he was a potter himself. In a brilliant leap of imagination, this inventor took two wheels, set them on their edges, and attached them to opposite ends of a pole, which led to the creation of the first cart.

When someone thought of adding two more wheels, the first wagon came into existence. Pulled by donkeys or oxen, wagons could hold heavier loads than a man or woman could lift—and more than a donkey could carry on its back. The first wagon may have been built as early as 3100 BCE. Now it was much easier for a craftsman to transport his goods.

Someone who wanted to sell or trade something needed a way to label the goods. Let's say, for example, that a Mesopotamian date grower wanted to ship his fruit to another town. He needed to identify his own jars, but he also wanted to make sure that no one stole any fruit before it reached the buyer. So he filled a large jar with dates and covered it with cloth or a baked-clay lid. Then he wrapped a string around the rim of the jar and pressed a blob of soft clay against the string. Finally, he made a label with a cylinder seal—a tube of carved stone or baked clay that could be rolled across the clay, creating a one-of-a-kind design. These designs were often beautiful, but they weren't just for show. They identified the owner of the goods and sealed the shipment against the greedy fingers of thieves.

All these new technologies were part of an even bigger change that was going on in southern Mesopotamia. The towns were growing larger all the time. By 3500 BCE, some of them can be called cities. One sprawling city, Uruk,

Donkeys pull a chariot with four solid wheels made of wood (top row).

which was near Eridu in modern-day Iraq, had grown to a population of more than 10,000 people—twice as big as any other Mesopotamian city that we know of at the time. Uruk's streets were full of people, donkeys, and wagons, and lined with brick houses jammed together on both sides. A vast temple complex dominated the town center. In fact, the remains found at Uruk are so impressive, archaeologists call this period of Mesopotamian history the "Uruk period."

Uruk's citizens must have shared certain duties, such as cleaning out the canals that brought water to the fields around the city and building places to worship together. Someone must have organized the people in order to get the work done. These men may have been the religious leaders who appear in the artwork of the Uruk period wearing beards, round hats, and thick belts.

The fact that some houses were bigger than others and some tombs were more elaborate suggests the development of a class system—including rich people who owned much of the property, a middle class of artisans and merchants, poor people who worked as small farmers, servants, and hired laborers, and perhaps even slaves. With the fertile fields producing more food than people needed to eat, those families with more land than others became rich.

The rich people wanted to trade for beautiful things:

Each of the round tiles in this wall from a temple at Uruk is made of painted clay. Although they look flat, they are actually cone shaped. The point of the cone sticks into the mortar. Together, these small tiles create a colorful pattern called a mosaic.

objects made of gold, silver, ivory, fine wood, and stone. To obtain these goods, some Mesopotamian traders in these early times traveled all the way to Egypt—a journey of about 1,500 miles. We know this because archaeologists have found Mesopotamian cylinder seals there and because Mesopotamian boats appear in some Egyptian art from the time.

Mesopotamia also sent out **colonists** to other parts of the Near East. Archaeologists have excavated cities in Syria that were almost identical to Mesopotamian cities built in the same period. The style of the houses and even the pottery used there were the same. Why did the Mesopotamians build these new cities? Was Mesopotamia becoming too crowded? Probably not. More likely, the Mesopotamians wanted greater control over trade. Setting up colonies in other places made it easier for them to get the luxury goods that they wanted.

Historians sometimes disagree on exactly what a community has to have or do in order to be called a "civilization." But most would agree that by the Uruk period, around 3500 BCE, the Mesopotamians had all the puzzle pieces in place. In fact, they were the first known people on Earth to "put it all together." They had cities that were organized under some kind of government. The remnants of their towering temples prove that they had organized religious practices. Within the community, some workers had begun to specialize—including priests, builders, potters, metalworkers and the stone-carvers who made cylinder seals. They sponsored long distance trade, and within the community there was a difference between rich and poor. Some scholars say that a culture must have a system of writing in order to be called a civilization, and that too was on its way in Mesopotamia.

Colonists leave home as an organized group to create a new community elsewhere, carrying their traditions with them. The ancient Greeks formed colonies throughout the Mediterranean and the Near East. In the 1600s and 1700s, European colonists settled in the Americas.

HOW ABOUT A DATE?

Just after World War II, chemist Willard F. Libby came up with carbon dating, a way of figuring out exactly how old is "old." He based his method on the fact that all living things have carbon in them. When a plant or animal dies, the radioactive part of its carbon—the part that produces energy in some form—begins to disappear, *very* slowly and always at the same rate. If a bone fragment is found in an ancient pot, carbon dating can tell us how long the animal has been dead by measuring the amount of radioactive carbon that is still left. Libby's method works on ancient animal remains up to 70,000 years old.

CHAPTER 4

❝ A MESSENGER TABLET AND A PERSONAL LETTER

HOW WORDS CHANGED THE WORLD
THE INVENTION OF WRITING

I n November 1989, astronaut Sonny Carter took a clay tablet with him on the space shuttle *Discovery*. Written in Mesopotamia in 2040 BCE, this tablet is the oldest human artifact ever to have traveled in space. It lists what six ancient travelers took as they began a long journey:

> For Bama, Baza the servant, Lugal-shazu, and Mash (each): 5 quarts of beer; 5 quarts of bread; 5 portions of onions; 3 portions of oil; and 2 portions of alkali.

❝ Messenger tablet, Iraq, 2040 BCE

> For Shu-Eshdar: 10 quarts of beer; 10 quarts of bread; 5 portions of onions; 3 portions of oil; and 2 portions of **alkali**.

> For Ubarum: 3 quarts of beer; 2 quarts of bread; 5 portions of onions, 3 portions of oil, 2 portions of alkali.

Alkalis are mineral salts found in soil, including desert sands. Dissolved in water, they can be used as soap.

> Month: cutting of the grain, 24th day, in the year that Huhnuri was raided.

Shu-Eshdar must have been the leader of the group. His rations of bread and beer were double those for Bama, Baza, Lugal-shazu, and Mash. Poor Ubarum must have been considered the least important. His rations included only three quarts of beer and two quarts of bread. The date on the tablet tells us that the travelers made their journey in the month when the grain is cut and in the year when the city of Huhnuri was raided. That's how the ancient Mesopotamians recorded years: pinning the time to an event. People still do that sometimes. You might say, for example, that your cousin was born on the same day and year that Saddam Hussein was captured in Iraq, which would mean December 15, 2003.

Astronaut Sonny Carter made history when he took a 4,000-year-old clay tablet from Mesopotamia into outer space in 1989.

The ancient words on the tablet that traveled with the astronauts were written more than four thousand years ago, but writing had already been in use for more than one thousand years by then. People had begun to speak long, long before writing was invented, though it's impossible to say exactly when or why. We do know, though, about the origins of writing in the Near East.

Imagine a primitive farmer living in a village in the green hills of northern Mesopotamia, around 8000 BCE. Each morning he leads his herd of 15 sheep to graze beneath shady oak and pistachio trees. One day, this farmer decides to send six of his sheep to his brother in a neighboring village, hoping for one of his brother's oxen in exchange. He sends a neighbor boy as his messenger. What if this boy delivers the sheep but forgets to ask for the ox? What if one of the sheep wanders off and is lost? Or what if the boy steals a sheep and sells it? Who would know? The brothers couldn't send written messages to each other to arrange the exchange because writing hadn't been invented yet.

People *had* figured out some ways of keeping records, though. The earliest farmers in the Near East kept track of business using tokens, which were small objects made of baked clay. Archaeologists have found thousands of tokens—red, brown, and gray ones, and round, oval, square, and even pot-shaped ones. One shape might represent a bushel of barley. Another might represent a pitcher of oil or a certain kind of animal. Some were only one centimeter across, while others were twice that size.

Suppose that the farmer used 15 tokens to stand for the 15 animals in his herd. He probably kept the tokens in a pottery jar. When a lamb was born, the farmer would drop another token into the jar. When he sent sheep to his brother, he'd throw away the same number of tokens. Or perhaps he'd send them along with the messenger.

For more than four thousand years, the token system

The Mesopotamians used small clay tokens to keep track of various goods, such as animals or jars of oil. The circular token with a cross on it (top) represented one sheep.

worked in this very simple way. But around 3350 BCE, about the same time that the first cities were growing in Mesopotamia, people devised a new system. Imagine another farmer now, living much later than the first one. Suppose that he, too, wanted to send six sheep to his brother in another village. This second farmer took six circular tokens with crosses on them and put them into a hollow ball of clay—an ancient envelope. Then he sealed the clay container with his cylinder seal—a tube of carved stone that created a unique design in the clay—and baked the whole thing in the sun. After the envelope hardened, he gave it to a messenger to take to his brother, along with the sheep.

When the messenger arrived, the brother would break open the clay ball. If he found six tokens, but counted only four sheep at his front door, he would demand to know about the missing sheep. The messenger still had to remember to ask for the ox. That kind of message couldn't be recorded yet, but communication had taken a giant step forward. Messages were traveling long-distance for the first time. And the idea spread. Clay balls with tokens still tucked inside have been found all over the ancient Near East.

People were communicating with one another through the clay envelopes, but they weren't writing yet. Their messages became clearer and more permanent when some clever person pressed one token onto a soft clay ball six times before baking it. Now there were no tokens to lose, and the message couldn't be changed easily. In time, the envelope balls were replaced by flat rectangular or pillow-shaped tablets that listed the numbers and amounts of various things. Now the farmer's brother could "read" the message that came along with the sheep. Better still, he could keep the tablet as a reminder to thank his brother when he saw him next.

After a while, someone realized that it was easier and quicker to draw the shape of the token. In keeping with Mesopotamian tradition, this person used what nature offered. Clay became his paper, and sharpened reeds from the riverbank became his pens. A farmer could write the symbols for *six*, *sheep*, *one*, and *ox* on his clay tablet. He still

The sign made of two wavy lines in the first row of this tablet is a pictogram that means "water."

couldn't write the words for *send, brother,* or *please.* But he was making progress.

Eventually people began to draw pictures of all sorts of things, such as a man, a tree, a star, or a foot. These drawings, called pictograms, mark the beginning of writing in Mesopotamia.

In time, the Mesopotamians found more and more words that they wanted to write. So they invented more and more pictures. At first, all the pictures represented *things*—nouns. But in time they came up with pictures for other parts of speech, such as verbs and adjectives. For example, if you were writing English with pictograms and drew a hand, it could represent the thing at the end of your arm. But it could also be used as a verb: *Hand* me the ball. Or it could be the first half of the word *hand*ball.

By 3200 BCE, the Mesopotamians were using hundreds of pictures in their writing. It must have been hard to remember them all. But the thrill of communicating in writing for the first time must have been like the excitement people felt when the telephone was invented in the mid-1870s and, for the first time, they were able to hear distant voices through the receiver.

Before long, simple words weren't enough. Ancient writers figured out a clever new "trick." Instead of having one sign that stood for one thing, such as the sun or a goat, they began to use pictures to represent the *sound* of a spoken word. This worked well because most Sumerian words were only one syllable long. A simple drawing could stand for a simple sound, such as *ga* (milk) or *lu* (man).

It also helped that the language had lots of homonyms—words that sound alike but have different meanings. The Sumerian word *ti,* for example, had three meanings: "life," "take," and "arrow." One of these words, *arrow,* is easy to

NOT-SO-DEAD DEAD LANGUAGES

Sumerian has not been spoken for four thousand years. But scholars of language have discovered its secrets by studying clay tablets and inscriptions written in ancient times. Sumerian is not related to any modern language. Akkadian, the other major language once spoken in Mesopotamia, is in the Semitic language family. This means that it is related to Hebrew, the language of ancient Jews and modern Israelis, and to Arabic, which is widely spoken in the Middle East today.

draw. So the Mesopotamians drew an arrow for all three words and let its use show the meaning. They also used the sign just for the sound "ti" when it appeared in any word. With this new method, the Mesopotamians could write almost anything: verbs, names, adjectives, even ideas such as love or fear.

About this same time, the signs became less like pictures and more like designs. Instead of drawing pictures in the clay, the writers began to create images by pressing the sharp ends of their reeds into the clay. Now all the lines in a sign were straight, made from the tip of the reed. Because the reeds were cut at an angle, the marks were wedge-shaped. We call this cuneiform writing, from the Latin word *cuneus*, which means "wedge." (The tablet that Sonny Carter took into space was written with cuneiform signs.)

Many ancient languages used the cuneiform script that the Sumerians invented, just as English, German, French, Spanish, Italian, and many other languages use the same alphabet. Each sign in the cuneiform script represented a syllable, so the script is known as a syllabary, not an alphabet. The Sumerians didn't think of representing each consonant with a single sign, as we do in our alphabet. So they needed many more than 26 phonetic signs.

Writing was a wonderful new tool, but it was still very complicated, with about six hundred cuneiform signs in regular use. Only a few people in each community actually learned to read and write. These were the scribes who did the writing for the whole community. Later some professionals such as judges and priests also learned to write.

It took hundreds of years for people to realize how helpful writing could be. At first, city leaders used it only for making lists: keeping track of taxes and trade. But scribes gradually found more and more uses for cuneiform. They began to write legal contracts, lists of words, hymns, prayers, and inscriptions for kings who wanted their names and deeds to be known by the gods and by people in future generations. But scribes never wrote diaries, biographies, news stories, or histories, which is a shame. We could have learned so much about their lives if they had.

MEANWHILE IN EGYPT...

The Mesopotamians weren't the only ones who invented writing. At about the same time, 3200 BCE, the Egyptians were inventing their own writing system, a collection of signs called "hieroglyphs." At first, each picture represented one word. Later, pictures came to represent sounds. Mesopotamia and Egypt were trading partners at that time, so it's possible that the Mesopotamians influenced the Egyptians. Or was it the other way around?

Writing also developed in South Asia and in China around this same time, but the dates are uncertain. Scholars of language are debating the issue now. Four lands—Iraq, Egypt, China, and the Indus Valley of South Asia—all claim to be the home of the earliest writing on earth.

Educated Mesopotamians finally began to write letters around 2400 BCE, and several hundred years later, ordinary people began to hire scribes to write special letters for them. Like most Mesopotamian letters, this letter found in Iraq begins with a wish for good health from the gods: "Tell Luga: Sin-putram sends the following message: May the gods...keep you in good health." Sin-putram wrote "tell Luga" because he knew Luga couldn't read and would have hired a scribe to read the message to him.

Finally, after thousands of years, by about 1700 BCE, a farmer could explain clearly to his brother that he was sending him six sheep and that he would like an ox in exchange. This was quite an accomplishment, but it would

66 Personal letter, Iraq, 18th or 17th century BCE

FROM PICTURES TO CUNEIFORM WRITING

ENGLISH WORD	AROUND 3100 BCE	AROUND 3000 BCE	AROUND 2500 BCE	AROUND 2100 BCE	AROUND 700 BCE
bread					
carp					
cow					
eat					
head					
plow					

Pictograms sometimes are recognizable as pictures of things, such as a face, a bowl, or a fish. But, over time, the symbols became simpler and could no longer be recognized as objects.

CUNEICODE

Each cuneiform sign represents at least one syllable, and most could be read in more than one way. The system worked well for writing Akkadian, since most Akkadian words include many vowels but not many clusters of consonants. It's hard to write English words using this syllabary, though. Akkadian had no *th*, *f*, *j*, *o*, *v*, or *y* sounds, and it never put more than two consonants together. To use cuneiform to write words in English, you need to add letters, insert vowels, and change some consonants. For example, it's easy to write the name Emily (e-mi-li) or Michael (mi-ka-el) but much harder to write Joseph (perhaps i-u-se-ip) or Stephanie (se-te-ip-ha-ni). The English word "sixths," with four consonants in a row, would have completely stumped an Akkadian scribe.

be a long time before an ordinary person could read or write. These skills were still in the hands of the lucky few.

Think about your day so far. How many times have you used your ability to read and write? Maybe you woke up to your alarm and read the time on a digital clock. At breakfast you may have read the words on the cereal box. Perhaps you read the headlines in the newspaper. Words and numbers cover our world—on street signs, on your computer screen, on buses and trains, and in books such as this one. We take writing so much for granted in our daily lives that we barely notice how much we read.

Writing, like the wheel or the plow, was once a new technology, an invention that allowed people to do things that hadn't been possible before. It allowed them to remember events without having to memorize them and to communicate over long distances. Once writing was invented—not just in Mesopotamia but also in Egypt, China, South Asia, and Mesoamerica—it was a revolution.

SOME CUNEIFORM SOUNDS AND SIGNS

SOUND	SIGN	SOUND	SIGN
e		li	
el		mi	
ha		ni	
i		se	
ik		si	
ip		te	
is		ti	
ka		u	

CHAPTER 5

A WORLD FULL OF GODS AND GODDESSES
RELIGION IN MESOPOTAMIA

❝ HYMNS TO THE GODS SHAMASH AND ENLIL, "INCANTATION AGAINST THUNDER," AND "MYTH OF ATRAHASIS"

The bright, shining ball that appeared each morning in the east, then climbed into the sky to give light and warmth to the world awed the Mesopotamians. They marveled as it disappeared in the west at night, only to reappear the next morning in the east. Had it traveled underground through the night? They called this powerful force *Utu* in the Sumerian language of southern Mesopotamia and *Shamash* in Akkadian, a language spoken in central Mesopotamia. We translate these words as *sun*.

Like all Mesopotamian gods, Shamash wears a horned helmet. The sun's rays flowing from his shoulders proclaim him the god of the sun. The seal at the right was rolled on clay to make the picture at the left.

The Mesopotamians found the sun mysterious. Where, they wondered, did its power come from? It seemed to move on its own, as people do. So it must be like a person in some ways, they reasoned. Their pictures of mighty Shamash show him as a man with curly hair and a beard, with the sun's rays radiating from his shoulders. They worshiped him with songs of praise:

> Of all the lands of different languages,
> You know their intentions, you see their footprints.
> All humankind kneels before you,
> O Shamash, everyone longs for your light.

❝ "The Shamash Hymn," Iraq, about 1500 to 1000 BCE

The Mesopotamians realized that Shamash was more than a large human being, though. For one thing, the sun didn't die—people had been seeing the same sun rise and set for generations. Also, the sun seemed to see everything. Its rays touched every part of the earth and shone on every-

The Great Flood

*The flood came forth,
Its destructive power came
 upon the peoples like a
 battle.
One person did not see
 another,
They could not recognize
 each other in the catastro-
 phe.
The deluge bellowed like
 a bull,
The wind resounded like a
 screaming eagle.*

"Myth of Atrahasis,"
17th century BCE

one, good and bad. The Mesopotamians came to think of Shamash as a wise and mighty judge who punished evildoers and rewarded those who lived good lives.

The Mesopotamians were polytheists, which means that they believed in many gods, not just Shamash. They reasoned that the gods must have different personalities, just as people have. They believed that each god controlled some part of the universe. Events on Earth occurred because the gods willed them. These beliefs helped the Mesopotamians to understand both the good and bad things that happened to them. When good things happened, they figured the gods must be happy. When bad things happened, it meant that one of the gods was upset.

In Mesopotamia, rainstorms were (and are) rare, but dramatic. A gathering storm can be seen far in the distance. The undersides of the clouds droop in big, angry-looking rolls. The wind builds up and sweeps huge gray-green clouds across the sky. Long before the thunder cracks, lightning shoots like arrows toward the ground. And then sheets of rain pull a thick curtain of water across the land.

The Mesopotamians believed that fierce Adad created these storms. You could actually see him fighting against Shamash, the sun god, as the clouds hid the sun and the

This broken tablet, written in Sumerian around 1740 BCE, describes the terrible winds and rains of a Great Flood that the Mesopotamians believed swept the whole Earth far back in their history. Only one man and his family survived.

In this 19th-century engraving, a hurricane on the Tigris River wrecks a steamboat. This was the kind of storm that convinced the Mesopotamians of Adad's power.

thunder crashed. When a Mesopotamian stood in the doorway of his home, trying to stay dry as the rain pelted his courtyard, and covered his ears to drown out of the storm, it was obvious to him that two great forces—two gods—were at war. A nameless poet described Adad as the warrior-god

> Who overturns raging enemies, . . .
> The one who makes the lightning flash . . .
> Who forms clouds in the midst of heaven . . .
> The one whose shout makes the people speechless
>   with fear . . .

" "Incantation Against Thunder," Iraq, about 1500 to 1000 BCE

Ishtar, the goddess of love, was the most important Mesopotamian goddess. Her Sumerian name, Inanna, means "Lady of Heaven," which makes her sound gentle. She wasn't. She had a hot temper, craved power, and loved to watch soldiers in battle.

All these gods and goddesses belonged to a complicated family tree and were related to one another as fathers, mothers, sons, daughters, husbands, and wives. They argued, fell in love, got jealous, and consulted with one another, just as humans do.

For many centuries, the people believed that Enlil was the greatest of the gods, even more powerful than Shamash. A speech written sometime between 1500 and 1000 BCE describes him as a god who is a

> Noble sovereign, . . .
> Whose words cannot be altered . . .
> The command of whose lips no god can ignore, . . .
> You are the leader of heaven, . . . lord of the lands.

" "To Enlil," Iraq, about 1500 to 1000 BCE

GODS OF THE NEAR EASTERN WORLD

REALM	AKKADIAN NAME	SUMERIAN NAME
Leader of the gods	Ellil	Enlil
Sun, justice	Shamash	Utu
Moon	Sin	Nanna
Sky	Anu	An
Wind, storm, war	Adad	Ishkur
Love, war	Ishtar	Inanna
Water	Ea	Enki
Midwife of the gods	Mami	–
City of Ashur	Ashur	–
City of Babylon	Marduk	–

The kindest of all the Mesopotamian gods was Ea, the god of fresh, sweet water. In Mesopotamian legends, he was the one who watched out for humans. And it's easy to see how he got his reputation. Without the fresh water of rivers and springs, people couldn't water their fields and grow their crops—and they would die.

Despite their world crowded with gods, the Mesopotamians believed that there was once a time when there were no gods, no Earth, and no sky. Their legends don't actually explain how the earliest gods came to be, but Anu was one of the first. His name means "heaven," and he was the elderly father of all the gods. The first item on the gods' to-do list was to separate the Earth from the sky. Next, they built homes for themselves: the ancient temples. And then a mighty god (probably Enlil) placed the stars and the moon in their proper places in the sky. This god made the clouds and set loose the Euphrates and Tigris, allowing them to flow through the river valley.

It would seem that the gods had all they needed to live

comfortably. But, unfortunately, they still had to plant seeds, harvest crops, and bake bread. Worst of all, they had the constant work of feeding and serving Enlil, their leader. Because the Mesopotamians believed that the gods had the same feelings as human beings do, it was logical to believe that the gods would become angry when they were over-worked. A story known as the Myth of Atrahasis, written down around the 17th century BCE, tells why the gods decided to create humankind.

> Great indeed was the drudgery of the gods, . . .
> They were complaining, denouncing,
> Muttering down in the ditch.

"Myth of Atrahasis," Iraq, 17th century BCE

The lesser gods ganged up on their lazy leader, Enlil. They would have killed him, but his doorkeeper warned him: "Enlil, your house is surrounded. Battle has run right up to your gate." When Enlil asked the other gods what was wrong, they complained that they had *had it* with work! Fortunately for Enlil, the kind god Ea saved the day. He came up with a compromise that satisfied all the gods. He suggested that they create a new creature to do all the work.

Ea asked Mami, the midwife of the gods, to create human beings. Mami agreed and suggested that Ea get her some clay so that she could create this new being. She took the clay, mixed it with the blood of a god, and made the first humans. Because the ancient Mesopotamians believed that the gods had created human beings to keep the gods happy, they accepted this as their main purpose in life: to feed, clothe, and shelter the gods. If they served well, they believed that their gods would let them live and prosper. But if they neglected the gods, the gods would grow angry, and the people would pay the price—suffering disease, bad luck, or even death.

The Mesopotamians believed that their gods were always close by. In fact, their view of the universe was pretty cozy. They imagined the earth as a big, flat circle with the Tigris and Euphrates rivers running through the middle. Their own land made up most of the world. A great salty sea circled the land on all sides. They believed that the Upper

A DAGGER DIVIDES THE WORLD

In one Mesopotamian myth, Marduk, god of the city of Babylon, created the world after defeating an evil goddess named Tiamat. Marduk killed the goddess, split her body in two, and turned the pieces into the earth and the sky. He created humans from the blood of an evil god who had sided with Tiamat.

The circle at the bottom of this cuneiform tablet shows a world map. It includes Babylon (the rectangle at the center), the Euphrates River (the two lines running through Babylon), and a circular sea, surrounding what the Mesopotamians thought was the whole world.

TWO BIRTHDAYS A YEAR?

The moon and stars helped Mesopotamian astronomers to create their calendar. They divided the year into days and months, just as we do, and measured their months by the phases of the moon. Each month began with the first glimpse of the new moon.

Although the Mesopotamian calendar had 12 months in the year, their year ended up being 11 days shorter than the solar year, which, as their astronomers knew, was 365 days long. So every few years, the king would just repeat a month so that the beginning of spring would show up in the right month—Nisannu. (The Mesopotamians didn't celebrate birthdays as we do today. If they had, a person occasionally would get to celebrate his birthday twice in one year.)

Sea (the Mediterranean) in the north was connected to the Lower Sea (the Persian Gulf) in the south by distant seas on the east and west.

We can guess that they thought the world was about five hundred miles across. Because they could travel only by walking, riding a donkey, or taking a boat, it would take weeks, or even months, to cover this distance. So to them, this world was enormous. When kings began to rule in Mesopotamia, they often called themselves kings "of the four rims of the universe" because they thought that Mesopotamia made up most of the universe.

Were the Mesopotamians foolish to envision such a small universe? Not at all. People living in 3000 BCE would never have seen a telescope, a globe, or even an atlas. And they certainly couldn't look down on the world's terrain from an airplane. All they knew were their own towns, the nearby villages, the river and canals that ran through the countryside, and maybe even a distant town that took several days to reach. For them, the universe was the world they could see, covered by an arching dome of sky.

Today we know that the earth moves around the sun. But the ancient Mesopotamians had no modern maps and science. All they had to go on was the evidence of their own eyes. And their eyes told them that the sun moves around the earth—as do the moon, planets, and all the stars. The sun, rising and setting, gave them proof each day. They "knew" that the gods who had created the world showed their great power in the brightness of the sun, in the fierceness of storms, and in the life-giving water of the rivers. No wonder they believed that Earth was the center of creation and their own land, the hub of the universe.

CHAPTER 6

THE DEATH OF A SUMERIAN LADY
QUEENS, KINGS, AND RELIGION IN EARLY CITIES

Rows of necklaces covered Queen Puabi's corpse from her neck to her waist, like a cloak. She wore gold earrings, and her headdress was made of gold ribbons and pendants. Treasures filled her burial room: a golden bowl, clay jars for food, silver lamps, two silver tables, the sculpted head of a cow in silver, and shells containing a green paint—most likely a cosmetic. Puabi must have been very, very rich. Her cylinder seal—the clay stamp that she used to sign her name—showed a banquet scene with people holding cups and the words *Puabi, nin. Nin* meant queen in Sumerian.

In 4,500 years, Puabi's tomb had never been looted by grave robbers. It was not until 1927 that the British archaeologist Sir Leonard Woolley and his team of archaeologists excavating the ancient Sumerian city of Ur found her skeleton resting peacefully among her burial gifts. Woolley wrote in his book on the excavation that she had been buried with "a gold cup in her hand; the upper part of [her] body was entirely hidden by a mass of beads of gold, silver, [and brightly colored stones]."

❝ Puabi's headdress from Ur, Iraq, 2500 BCE

The weight of earth in a royal tomb crushed this skull, but the body's remains are still adorned with a head-dress, necklace, and earrings.

They found that the ancient queen, who stood less than five feet tall, had good teeth. This probably means that she didn't eat many sweets and that her bread didn't have much sand in it, which was a problem for poorer people whose flour contained stone dust from the grindstones. Her leg bones show that she spent a lot of time squatting on her heels. Was this how she usually sat?

Two female servants were buried with Puabi, and outside the actual tomb were dozens more skeletons, mostly women. Beautifully dressed and

Leonard Woolley—wearing a suit and surrounded by his wife and local workmen—sits on the ground and records his finds during the excavations at Ur. Archaeologists no longer dress so formally. Suits are definitely out these days.

bejeweled, these people seemed to have just slumped down. Small cups lay near their bodies. Archaeologists believe that they all drank poison in order to follow Puabi into the afterlife. Among the dead was a young musician whose fingers still touched the strings of a small hárp. Did she die while playing for Puabi's funeral? Were Puabi's attendants willing to die with her? Were they servants and slaves or members of the royal court?

Puabi was probably the wife or mother of a king or she may have been a priestess who was called a "nin" because of her great power and wealth. Women held some of the highest positions in Mesopotamia from around 2600 to 2300 BCE. This was unusual among ancient civilizations and it continued for hundreds of years. Mesopotamian women eventually lost some of their rights and privileges, but no one knows why.

Puabi was not the only person from Ur to have others buried with her. In the century and a half from 2600 to 2450 BCE, 15 royals were accompanied in death by attendants—74 were found in one royal tomb! The things buried with these attendants—such as lyres, chariots, spears, and axes—tell us that the dead included musicians, soldiers, grooms for the animals, and perhaps ministers of the household.

There were no gold or silver mines in Mesopotamia. So the presence of these valuable metals in Puabi's tomb proves that the people of Ur were already linked with trading partners spread across the Near East. Traders must have brought these raw materials—gold, silver, bronze, and gems—from other places so that local artists and craftsmen could create beautiful jewelry, furniture, grand chariots, and sculpture for wealthy people such as Puabi.

Beginning around 2900 BCE, kings had begun to rule in the southern part of Mesopotamia, which is known as Sumer. And by Puabi's time (about 2500 BCE), kings ruled each of Sumer's major cities, including Ur. Some of the kings had the title *lugal*, which means "big man." Lugal became the Sumerian word for king. Perhaps, at first, these men served just during wartime and only later began to rule full time. Scholars would love to know for sure.

THE WILD AND WOOLLEY EAST

The phrase "wild and woolly" usually describes a rambunctious person or a place where unexpected excitement is on the menu every day. When the British archaeologist Leonard Woolley was on the scene, it was usually that way. Woolley explored Roman ruins, spied for the British Foreign Office during World War I, and later worked as an archaeologist in the Middle East. When a member of his archaeological team found something important, he rewarded the person with cash and shot off a round of rifle fire to celebrate.

From 1922 to 1934, Woolley excavated the Sumerian city of Ur with the unusual combination of great patience and boundless energy. He and his team uncovered many of the city's secrets, from its earliest reed huts to its great ziggurat—a temple tower built around 2000 BCE.

❝ Sumerian King List, Iraq, around 2100 BCE

❝ Stone bowl from Khafaje, Iraq, around 2600 BCE

❝ Royal Inscription of Eannatum, Iraq, around 2400 BCE

A Mesopotamian scribe, writing about 2100 BCE, named some of the early kings on a cuneiform tablet known as the Sumerian King List. He wrote that the idea of kingship was a gift from the gods: "When kingship was lowered from heaven, kingship was first in Eridu," one of the earliest inhabited cities in Mesopotamia.

According to the King List, the first rulers had unbelievably long reigns: "A-lulim [became] king and ruled 28,800 years. Alalgar ruled 36,000 years." By the time the list was written, the first kings had been dead for centuries. In people's minds, these kings had become superheroes who had lived almost forever. (They hadn't, of course. Almost no one on Earth has ever lived to be more than about 120.) The King List describes each king as having ruled the whole land from a particular city, though in fact no king really controlled more than the land around his capital at this time.

The earliest known royal inscription—a king's proclamation of his greatness—written about 2600 BCE, was by a king who had his name etched on a stone bowl. It read, simply: "Mebaragesi, King of Kish," an early Mesopotamian city. Mebaragesi was the first king that we know of to use *writing* to mark his existence and his place in the world. The Sumerian King List records his name, but adds *en*, a title of respect that meant "lord": "En-mebaragesi, the one who carried away as spoil the weapons of the land of Elam, became king, and reigned 900 years." Elam was a land to the east of Mesopotamia and a long-time enemy of the Mesopotamians.

Kish and Ur were not the only powerful cities in Sumer from 2900 to 2300 BCE. Many small kingdoms dotted the region (modern Iraq), each with a king and his government. Excavations in a city-state called Lagash have uncovered cuneiform texts and inscriptions that tell us more about current events there than any other Sumerian city.

Several inscriptions describe the adventures of Eannatum, a king of Lagash who bragged that "Eannatum, ruler of Lagash, [was] granted strength by Enlil, nourished with special milk by [the goddess] Ninhursag, [and] given a fine name by [the

Eannatum's soldiers carry identical weapons and wear matching helmets. Marching in formation, with their shields overlapping and spears ready for battle, they would have terrified their enemies.

FUZZY DATES

Scholars are not certain about the dates of events in ancient Near Eastern history until about 1000 BCE. Ancient kings used lots of different ways of dating the years in their reigns, and historians try to pin down these dates by connecting them to our modern way of numbering the years. There are several ways to do this: by comparing the histories of two different peoples and by comparing written documents with the evidence found by archaeologists, geologists, astronomers, and chemists. The dates given in this book are the ones that historians have decided to use for now, but they might be wrong, perhaps by as much as one hundred or even two hundred years in some places. The order of events and kings is right, though.

god] Nanshe." He claimed that the gods had always been on his side. The clay tablets found in his cities also tell us a lot about the wars that he fought and the way he organized his kingdom. The scribes kept track of everything.

As the Sumerian cities of southern Mesopotamia became richer, better organized, and more warlike, they also became better protected. Their leaders built high walls around the cities and fortified the city gates. In order to build walls, palaces, and temples and to dig canals, the kings almost certainly called upon the residents for their labor. Men were probably drafted to work for a given time on community projects. The royal household used cuneiform tablets to list the workers' names, the days of their service, and the amount of barley that each one was given.

Some of the first organized governments in the world were born in these early Sumerian city-states, and this is one of ancient Mesopotamia's great legacies. The Mesopotamian kings were among the first leaders who tried to convince their people that they really *needed* kings and that the gods

A musician and a singer entertain the king (top, left), as guests at his banquet toast their host. People bring gifts to the king (lower rows) in this mosaic called the Standard of Ur.

CHANGE ALL THE HISTORY BOOKS!

Until late in the 20th century, historians of the Near East writing about the third millennium BCE (the 2000s) focused mostly on Mesopotamia. They believed that the rest of the region had only small farming villages at that time. Recently, though, excavations in Syria have shown that small kingdoms flourished there at the same time as the city-states in Mesopotamia. They, too, had local kings, trading networks, and armies.

liked the idea, too. Kings were especially useful when foreign enemies attacked. Sometimes cities in southern Mesopotamia joined together to fight a common enemy, but it would be many years before any city became strong enough to force the others into forming a single kingdom under a single ruling power.

Although the governments of these cities were independent of one another at this time, their people had a lot in common. They shared the same religion. They spoke the same languages: Sumerian in the south and Akkadian farther north. (In many cities, people spoke both languages.) What's more, they built their houses and temples in the same ways, they ate from the same types of pottery, they used the same writing system, and they even wore the same styles of jewelry. Did ancient traveling salesmen market their wares by inviting the wealthy Mesopotamians to buy necklaces—just like the ones that Queen Puabi wore?

CHAPTER 7

THE FIRST SUPERHERO
THE STORY OF GILGAMESH

King Gilgamesh was the world's first super-hero. But not everything about him was heroic. In fact, at first, he wasn't someone you'd really want to know.

According to Mesopotamian legend, Gilgamesh ruled Uruk, one of the largest cities in Sumer, around 2600 BCE. The 12th-century BCE Babylonian poet Sin-leqe-unnini describes Gilgamesh as a wild, self-centered young man who ventured off with his best friend Enkidu to cedar forests hundreds of miles away from Uruk to fight a monster named Humbaba. Before the two left on their quest, Gilgamesh declared to his subjects,

> Hear me, O elders of Uruk-the-Town-Square.
> I want to tread the path to ferocious Humbaba...
> I will conquer him in the Forest of Cedar...
> I will establish forever a name eternal.

Gilgamesh wanted to be famous.

When the two friends found Humbaba, the monster begged for his life, but "Gilgamesh struck him in the neck, [and] Enkidu...pulled out the [monster's] lungs." When the heroes returned to Uruk, they entered the city gates in triumph. Even the goddess of love, Ishtar, was amazed and promptly fell in love with Gilgamesh. He must have thought he was as powerful as a god, because he not only rejected Ishtar, but he also insulted her. Ishtar "went up to heaven in a furious rage." She asked her father, the god Anu, to send the Bull of Heaven to punish Gilgamesh.

But again, Gilgamesh and Enkidu were victorious. They killed the fierce bull. Now *all* the gods were furious. Humans were not supposed to have this kind of power. Someone must pay for this crime. The gods punished Enkidu instead of Gilgamesh, and Enkidu became ill because of their curse.

Humbaba, the monster who controlled and guarded the Cedar Forest, bares his teeth. The Gilgamesh epic tells how Gilgamesh and Enkidu cut off Humbaba's head.

🙶 Sin-leqe-unnini, *The Epic of Gilgamesh*, 12th century BCE

One night, Enkidu saw in a dream what existence would be like after death. He told Gilgamesh that his dream had led him to "the house of darkness,...on the path that allows no journey back, to the house whose residents are deprived of light." He described the dismal life of the dead where "soil is their sustenance and clay their food, where they are dressed like birds in coats of feathers, and see no light, but dwell in darkness."

A few days after telling his dream to Gilgamesh, Enkidu died. Gilgamesh refused to allow his friend's body to be buried. He stayed by the deathbed, hoping that somehow Enkidu would miraculously come back to life. Later in the epic, Gilgamesh described his wait: "Enkidu, whom I love so much, who went through every hardship with me...Six days and seven nights I wept over him, I did not allow him to be buried until a worm fell out of his nose." Finally, Gilgamesh had to accept his friend's death, but he was heartbroken.

Gilgamesh began to long for immortality, the never-ending life that the gods enjoyed. He didn't want to die—ever. He began a life of wandering, looking for some way to escape death. During his travels, Gilgamesh met an innkeeper who told him that he would never find immortality. She advised him to just enjoy the simple things in life: "Let your belly be full,...dance and play day and night...Gaze on the child who holds your hand....For this is the destiny of mortal men."

Gilgamesh rejected the innkeeper's wise advice and continued his travels. Eventually he met a bearded old man named Utnapishtim, who answered

Sin-leqe-unnini, *The Epic of Gilgamesh*, 12th century BCE

Gilgamesh kills the monster Humbaba. Scholars believe that when a hero—rather than a king or a god—appears in ancient Mesopotamian art, it is usually Gilgamesh.

Gilgamesh's question about how to live forever with a long tale. He said that many, many years ago, the kind god Ea had warned him about a huge flood that was coming. Following Ea's orders, Ut-napishtim had built a huge boat and boarded it just before the **flood** began, saving himself, his family, and animals of every kind on Earth. Ut-napishtim then told Gilgamesh how the god Enlil, who had caused the flood, decided to give Ut-napishtim and his wife the gift of eternal life. Ut-napishtim explained, though, that Gilgamesh couldn't become immortal in the same way, because Enlil had promised that he would never again cover the earth with floodwater.

Ut-napishtim saw that Gilgamesh was determined to gain eternal life, so he gave him a test. He said that if Gilgamesh wanted to live forever, he would first have to stay awake for seven days and nights. Gilgamesh tried, but he failed completely. Instead of staying awake, he slept for the full seven days—proving to himself and Ut-napishtim that he was an ordinary mortal.

Ut-napishtim couldn't help Gilgamesh live forever, so he gave him a consolation prize: clues about where to find a plant that would make him young again. Gilgamesh found the magical plant, but carelessly left it lying around and a snake stole it. In the end, after all his adventures, Gilgamesh was no closer to eternal life than he had been at the start of his quest. But he may have gained a bit of wisdom.

Sin-leqe-unnini's version of the story ends with Gilgamesh going home. As his boat neared the shore, King Gilgamesh told the boatman about Uruk's beauty and impressive size: "three square miles and a half is Uruk's expanse." Gilgamesh finally realized that he could be content without immortal life.

Gilgamesh was a legendary character, and Mesopotamians had been telling tales and writing about him for 1,500 years before Sin-leqe-unnini recorded his adventures as a story-poem, or epic. Sin-leqe-unnini's poem was 3,000 lines long and covered 11 cuneiform tablets. It is the world's first-known epic. For centuries, professional storytellers performed at banquets and often must have told the tale of

Scientists have shown that no flood ever covered the entire Earth, but there's evidence in Mesopotamia of several huge floods long before writing was invented, and for the Mesopotamians, their land was the whole Earth.

VIEWS OF THE BEYOND

The Mesopotamians believed that the gods rewarded and punished people for good or bad behavior while they were still alive. Good people would have health, large families, and property, but the gods would punish the evil ones with sickness and early death. The afterlife, they believed, was a dark, grim place where people ate dirt. And everyone, good and bad, went there. The Hebrews, Greeks, and Romans also believed in a grim afterlife. Of the Mediterranean and Near Eastern peoples living before 600 BCE, only the Egyptians expected the afterlife to be a wonderful place—*if* the gods allowed you to go there.

EPIC EMOTIONS

The same problems that troubled Gilgamesh, the world's first superhero, turn up in later books and films. In the *Iliad*, a Greek epic written in the ninth century BCE, the hero Achilles is devastated because his friend has died. Achilles says, "Then let me die at once since it was not my fate to save my dearest comrade from his death!" In J. R. R. Tolkien's *Lord of the Rings*, Frodo—much like the innkeeper in Gilgamesh—reassures a friend whom he has to leave: "You cannot always be torn in two. You will have to be one and whole, for many years. You have so much to enjoy and to be, and to do." Like Gilgamesh, these characters all have to struggle with human mistakes and worries, which makes them stronger and wiser in the end.

Gilgamesh's name appears on the King List, which was written down five hundred years after Gilgamesh supposedly ruled. But no tablets dating from his reign have ever been found. Was Gilgamesh a real king?

A harpist (bottom row) entertains guests at a banquet. Perhaps he is singing the story of Gilgamesh. The plaque was made soon after the hero's lifetime.

Gilgamesh. Music would have accompanied the story, and some parts of it might have been sung. The Mesopotamians loved banquets. We know because Mesopotamian cylinder seals and other works of art show people at banquets where singers performed to music played on a lyre or harp, a flute, and a drum. Other musical instruments included lutes, horns, and clackers. Sometimes dancers performed at these events. The guests sat around large vases and sipped drinks though long straws made of reeds. They probably listened for hours to the exciting tales and the lively music, and may even have joined in, singing along to familiar sections and choruses.

The story of Gilgamesh is not just about an adventure. It's also a story about ideas. And people have been writing about these same thoughts, asking these same questions ever since. What is a hero? Why do people die? What is the meaning of friendship? How can we live our lives in the best way? The story of Uruk's ancient **king** brought these questions to people's minds. Did they talk about them as they sat together under the stars?

CHAPTER 8

THE WORLD'S FIRST EMPIRE BUILDER
SARGON, KING OF AKKAD

📖 AN AKKADIAN
LEGEND, SARGON'S
INSCRIPTIONS,
A SYRIAN LETTER,
AND "THE CURSE
OF AGADE"

📖 "The Legend of Sargon," Iraq,
first millennium BCE

My mother was a high priestess; I did not
know my father...
My mother... gave birth to me in secret.
She placed me in a reed basket; she sealed the hatch
  with tar.
She threw me in the river,
  which did not rise over me.

Who was this unwanted baby? When he was
born, his unwed mother set him adrift on the
river—he could easily have drowned. Perhaps,
by launching him in a waterproof basket-
boat, she hoped that someone would find him
and give him a better life than she could. And
that's what happened. He grew up to be Sargon
the Great.

According to the "The Legend of Sargon,"
an Akkadian story recorded on a clay tablet in
the first millennium BCE, the baby Sargon was
found by a laborer named Akki, a simple man
who filled the canals in a rich man's garden
with water:

The river carried me up and brought me
  to Akki, the water-drawer.
Akki, the water-drawer, lifted me up
  when he dipped in his bucket.
Akki, the water-drawer, took me as his
  son, and raised me.
Akki, the water-drawer, appointed me as his
  gardener,
and when I was a gardener, [the goddess] Ishtar
took a liking to me.

*Kings often wore a braided band
around their heads. Unlike earlier
Sumerian kings, this one sports a long
curly beard. He could be the great
Akkadian King Sargon.*

Sargon doesn't explain how he managed to trade a gardener's wagon for a royal chariot, except to say that, with Ishtar's backing, he became king over the "black-headed people." (The Mesopotamians always referred to themselves, and sometimes to all humankind, as "black-headed people.") Stories about Sargon, including the one about his birth, were written down hundreds of years after his reign. Historians consider them to be legends, not history. In addition to the legends about Sargon, surviving copies of his royal inscriptions prove that he did actually rule as king, that he came to power around 2340 BCE, and that he had one of the longest reigns of any Mesopotamian king: 56 years.

We don't know where Sargon grew up, but it must have been north of Sumer because Akkadian, not Sumerian, was his native language. His family is a mystery, too. We don't know his mother's name—only that she was a high priestess. And whoever his father was, he was probably not a king. Sargon almost certainly would have named him in his inscriptions, if he *had* been.

Sargon may have overthrown a ruling king and stolen his throne. We can't be sure. But the fact that he chose a new city, Agade, which was north of Sumer, as his capital supports the idea. Perhaps it was a way of saying that he was the new and rightful ruler of a brand-new kingdom.

During Sargon's long reign, he conquered all of Mesopotamia, from the Lower Sea all the way to the Upper Sea (from the Persian Gulf to the Mediterranean Sea). He created the first **empire** in history.

One inscription, describing his victory over the Sumerian city of Uruk, brags that he "tore down its wall," and brought its king "in a dog collar to the gate of [the god] Enlil." Another one, copied from a statue that was probably made in Sargon's own time, boasted that "Sargon,...was victorious in 34 battles and destroyed walls as far as the edges of the sea." Tearing down a city's walls meant the end of that city's safety and independence. This same inscription later mentions Sargon as a trader: "He had ships from Meluhha, Magan, and Dilmun moor at the piers of Agade." We know that the inscription was not an exaggeration—

Empires are bigger than kingdoms. An empire includes not only people of the same nationality as the king, but people with different languages and different traditions as well.

" Royal inscriptions, Iraq, about 2000 BCE

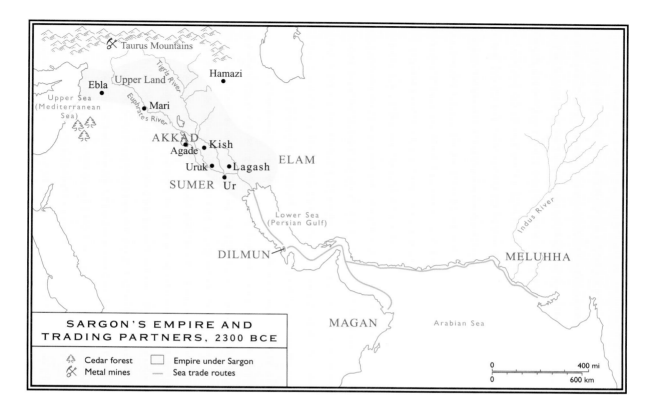

SARGON'S EMPIRE AND
TRADING PARTNERS, 2300 BCE

🌲 Cedar forest   ☐ Empire under Sargon
⛏ Metal mines   — Sea trade routes

Mesopotamian objects have been found in all these faraway
places. Traders would have traveled to Mesopotamia by
boat through the Persian Gulf.

When Sargon fought foreign enemies, he prayed to their
gods as well as his own. He believed a victory meant that
the foreign gods had been on his side. One of his inscriptions bragged that the local gods had given him valuable
lands in Syria and Lebanon: "the Upper Land, Mari, Yarmuti,
and Ebla, as far as the Cedar Forest and the metal mines."
After he conquered these regions that were rich in forests
and mines, Sargon no longer had to depend upon trade for
lumber and expensive metals. He could just order the conquered peoples to send these valuable goods as tributes to
his greatness.

Sargon's capital city of Agade has never been found. But
one of the cities that he claimed to have conquered, Ebla—
in Syria, far to the north of Akkad—has turned out to be a

❝ Royal inscription, Iraq,
about 2000 BCE

Thousands of years after the palace at Ebla burned down, archaeologists found these tablets still in rows. When the shelves burned, the tablets fell to the ground in order.

treasure trove of information. A team of Italian archaeologists discovered that a terrible fire destroyed Ebla's palace. (It might have been torched by conquerors, perhaps by Sargon himself.) But in a strange twist of fate, the fiercely burning fire saved 17,000 inscribed clay tablets, complete or in pieces, by baking them brick-hard. Some of the tablets were big: squares and rectangles as big as a sheet of notebook paper. Others were no bigger than a postage stamp, crowded with tiny cuneiform writing. These texts propel us back to life in an ancient Syrian palace and give us the clearest pictures we have of life in the Near East during the third millennium BCE.

Many of Ebla's texts are just lists, and reading them is about as thrilling as reading a phone book. Some, for instance, list the clothing that was handed out to thousands of people in the kingdom. But taken together, these texts show that, in any given year, more than five thousand workers, craftsmen, and officials received food, drink, and clothing from their king. The palace's metal workshops alone employed five hundred men, and hundreds of women spun and wove flax and wool into cloth for the palace. Almost everyone in Ebla depended upon the king and the palace.

Archaeologists also found some more exciting items, such as a letter written by a scribe named Tira-il. Ibubu, the palace steward, had summoned him to write to the king's representative in the distant town of Hamazi in northern Iran. When he received this message, Tira-il would have prepared a blank clay tablet and brought his stylus with him. He probably drew careful lines on the tablet before he left home and marked the columns in which he would later write. At the palace, Ibubu dictated, and Tira-il wrote:

> Thus says Ibubu, the steward of the palace of the king to the envoy [of the city of Hamazi]: I am your brother and you are my brother....Whatever desire you express, I shall grant you, [and] whatever desire I express, you shall grant....May you deliver to me the finest quality **equids**....I, Ibubu, have given you...ten wagon ropes and two...wagons.

Ibubu almost certainly didn't mean that he and the official from Hamazi were real brothers—it was just a way of saying that they should behave like brothers. Ibubu emphasized the friendship between the two towns by saying that not only were the messengers brothers, but so, also, were the kings: "the king of Ebla is the brother of...the king of Hamazi."

Tira-il, like all the scribes at Ebla, must have been trained to write in a local school for scribes. Archaeologists have found 40 tablets at Ebla with lists of Sumerian words. Their excavations have also uncovered tablets listing Sumerian words with their Eblaite translations—the earliest dictionaries known anywhere in the world.

Tira-il may have delivered his letter personally, because the king of Hamazi probably didn't know how to read. He, like the king of Ebla, depended on scribes such as Tira-il to read to him. But first, the scribe made a copy of his letter to keep in the files at Ebla, so that the king could remember what was sent, and this is what the archaeologists found.

Sumerian words are translated into the local language of Eblaite on this tablet, which is one of the world's earliest-known dictionaries.

❝ Letter, Syria, 24th century BCE

{ Equids are horses and other horselike animals, such as mules and donkeys. Ibubu was probably asking for donkeys, because horses had not yet been domesticated in the Near East.

Like the kings of Hamazi and Ebla, Sargon, too, must have sent his scribes to foreign courts. These messengers carried letters, luxury goods, and gifts—acting as ambassadors for their royal masters. They were the world's first **diplomats**, and Tira-il's letter, written on a clay tablet, is the first evidence of diplomacy in the history of the world.

Early diplomats wrote, traveled, and made deals between kingdoms or city-states. They represented the ruler, acting on his behalf.

Until it was destroyed, Ebla was a wealthy city. The lists show that huge amounts of silver, copper, gold, and clothing came into the palace every year. Ebla probably also grew rich from taxes on trade that passed through the city, which was on a well-traveled route from Mesopotamia to the Mediterranean Sea.

This tall monument celebrates the military victory of King Sargon's grandson, King Naram-Sin. The king's horned helmet means that he was presenting himself as a god—usually only gods wore horned helmets in Mesopotamian art.

The destruction of this thriving kingdom came quickly, around 2300 BCE. The scribes left no clues as to who was responsible. We know that Sargon brought his army to the region, but no one knows for sure whether or not he was the one who destroyed it.

Archaeologists have not yet found Sargon's own capital city, Agade. But in the "Curse of Agade," a document that archaeologists have pieced together from more than 30 fragments, ancient writers describe it as a fabulous place:

"The Curse of Agade," Iraq, 2000 BCE

[T]he dwellings of Agade were filled with gold,
Its bright-shining houses were filled with silver...
Inside, the city was full of ... music ... [and]
Its quays where the boats docked were all a-bustle.

Will archaeologists someday find Agade? How many other cities and kingdoms lie hidden beneath the sands and soils of Iraq and Syria, waiting to be discovered and reveal their secrets?

CHAPTER 9

THE CARE AND FEEDING OF ANCIENT GODS

PRIESTESSES AND PRIESTS IN MESOPOTAMIA

King Sargon chose his daughter, Enheduanna, for one of the most important jobs in all of Mesopotamia: high priestess in the temple of **Nanna**, god of the moon. Nanna's temple was in the walled city of Ur, one of the many cities that Sargon had conquered.

Obeying her father's wishes, Enheduanna left her home in Sargon's capital, Agade, and traveled to Ur, which was near the shore of the Gulf. She moved into the palace where Nanna's priestesses lived. From then on, she lived shut away from the day-to-day life of ordinary people. She wasn't allowed to marry. And although she probably lived in luxury with many servants to attend her, she herself was a servant in Nanna's "house."

Each day Enheduanna sang praises to Nanna and chanted prayers, begging him to support her family, especially her father, Sargon. She wrote some hymns herself and signed her name to them, making her the world's first known author. More than 50 cuneiform copies of one of her hymns (or parts of it) have been found and are in museums around the world. Not all Enheduanna's hymns were written to "her" god, Nanna. She also honored Inanna, the goddess of love. In one of her hymns to Inanna, Enheduanna says she hopes that Ashimbabbar, another name for Nanna, will not be jealous:

{ Many ancient gods had more than one name. The moon god was first called by his Sumerian name, Nanna, but he was also known as Ashimbabbar and later in Akkadian as Sin.

Enheduanna and her assistants stand before the altar of the god Nanna to perform their sacred duties. This alabaster disk was found in the palace where the high priestess lived.

📖 Enheduanna, "Hymn to
Inanna," around 2300 BCE

I, Enheduanna, will offer supplications to her,
My tears, like sweet drinks,
Will I present to the holy Inanna, I will greet her
   in peace,
Let not Ashimbabbar be troubled.

At this point in her life, Enheduanna was out of favor
at Ur—and out of a job. We don't know what the problem
was, but in her hymn to Inanna, she blames Nanna for her
troubles:

📖 Enheduanna, "Hymn to
Inanna," around 2300 BCE

As for me, my Nanna watched not over me,
I have been attacked most cruelly. . . .
I, . . . have been driven forth from my house, . . .
   forced to flee . . . like a swallow

Eventually, Enheduanna regained power and returned to
her duties in Nanna's temple. There she not only worshiped
him, she also bathed, dressed, and fed him. How could anyone have believed that a person could do these things for the
moon? To the Mesopotamians, the answer was simple: each
god and goddess had two forms. The first was the spirit of
the god as it lived in nature—Nanna in the sky, for instance,
or the god Ea who lived in fresh water. But gods and goddesses also lived in the temples that were dedicated to them.

The Mesopotamians believed that the spirit of each god
lived in a special statue, now called a cult statue. These statues, made in human form to represent the humanlike characters of the gods, had the same needs as any human. Not
only could they fall in or out of love, they could become
angry, tired, or hungry. So, each day Enheduanna and her
assistants fixed fine meals for Nanna and set them before
his statue. After Nanna had "eaten"—perhaps by absorbing
the smell of the food—the high priestess and other temple
workers ate and drank the meal.

No complete cult statues have survived. But we know
that they existed because ancient texts mention them and
because we have pictures of them in ancient sculpture and on
cylinder seals. The statues appear to have been made from
precious metals, such as bronze and gold, and decorated

*The eyes and hair on this marble head
would have been inlaid with precious
materials such as gold and lapis lazuli.
She probably represents a goddess.*

The hands of these figures are folded in prayer. Wealthy Mesopotamian men and women could dedicate such statues of themselves in local temples to pray for them and their families.

with semi-precious stones. In these ancient images, the gods and goddesses wear beautiful clothes and are often seated on thrones. All gods had horns on their headdresses— a decoration reserved for divine beings—and male gods were often shown wearing beards.

Why did Sargon send Enheduanna so far away? After Sargon had conquered the southern Sumerian cities and brought them into his empire, he seems to have decided that he wanted to control religion as well as politics in the far reaches of his kingdom. So he put his daughter in a high position to represent him in Ur, one of the largest and most important cities in the south.

Each major city was "home" to a particular god or goddess. **Nippur** was the city of Enlil, ruler of the Mesopotamian gods, and Ur belonged to Nanna, Enlil's son. Ever since the time of the earliest towns (5000 to 3800 BCE), the Mesopotamians had built temples on platforms that were sometimes as tall as a house. Kings often bragged about having restored or rebuilt a particular temple in order to please their city's god.

Temples, like palaces, owned fields, grazing lands, orchards, and irrigation canals. Many people lived and worked on temple-owned lands. These temple workers worked the soil, took care of the hundreds of sheep and goats, wove cloth and mats, made bread, brewed beer, and carved stone objects to glorify the gods. We know from cuneiform lists that other temple workers swept floors, carried buckets of water and fuel, and worked as security guards.

The priests and priestesses had the most important job

Because Nippur was Enlil's home city, Mesopotamians honored Nippur just as Catholics today respect Rome (where the Pope lives) and Muslims respect Mecca (the birthplace of Muhammad, Islam's founder).

Like most Mesopotamian temples, this one (by a modern painter) was built on a high platform in the city center. In it were courtyards, workshops, and storerooms, as well as the holy room where the cult statue was kept.

❝ List of omens, Iraq, 1st millennium BCE

of all: to serve and glorify the god or goddess, and each had particular duties. The purification priest had to make sure that the temple was free of ordinary dirt, but also clear of all wickedness and evil. Diviners, priests who were experts in divination, were supposed to figure out the will of the gods from signs such as a shooting star, an unusually bright planet, an eclipse of the sun, or the birth of a three-legged calf. To figure out the meaning of these signs (or omens), the diviner checked the records to see if this odd event had ever happened before, and if so, what had happened afterwards. One ancient tablet warned that if the stars of the constellation Orion sparkle brightly, "somebody influential will get too much power and will commit evil deeds."

A diviner also studied the innards of sacrificed animals—the liver of a sacrificed goat, for instance. He would compare the goat's bloody liver with others that had been copied and kept as clay replicas in the temple. The will of the god would then be "read" from the various bumps, hollows, and deformities that he found and interpreted.

As high priestess, Enheduanna didn't preach to a congregation because most worshippers weren't even allowed inside the temples. But a man or woman could have a small stone statue made in his or her image. This statue, showing the person praying to the god, would be placed near the god's statue to remind him to watch over the person and his family. This was possible only for the wealthy. Most people practiced their religion in their own homes, saying prayers to their personal gods and goddesses. A poem called "I Will Praise the Lord of Wisdom" describes a man whose string of bad luck convinced him that he had somehow neglected and angered the gods.

> Like one who has not . . . called upon his goddess
>   when he ate . . .
> Like one who has gone crazy and forgotten his lord, . . .
> Like such a one do I appear.

A religious Mesopotamian such as this poet would have followed daily rituals and celebrated all public holy days and festivals. He would have taught his children and servants to honor the gods. And he would never, ever have sworn to a false statement in the name of any god.

On festival days and holy days, priests carried the statues of the gods and goddesses through the streets of the city, and the people felt blessed simply by being there. Everyone had the day off work to join in the joyful celebration. But the high point of the year occurred when the gods went visiting. The cult statues were carried by boat to a neighboring city to express the friendship between the gods and their peoples. Everyone would celebrate with feasting, dancing, and socializing. The temple priests and priestesses organized these festivals for the gods and the people. Throughout her lifetime, Enheduanna must have presided over many of them in Nanna's city of Ur.

The position of high priestess at Ur stayed in Enheduanna's family for many years. The kings who followed Sargon, even when new dynasties came to the throne, continued to appoint women—their daughters or sisters—to serve as the high priestesses of Nanna. When these women died, they were buried in a special chamber under the palace. Grave robbers have stripped these tombs of their bones and burial treasures. Which tomb held the bones of Sargon's daughter, princess and priestess of Nanna? The thieves were thorough and left no clues.

" "I Will Praise the Lord of Wisdom," 13th century BCE

HONORING THE GODS

From the time of the Mesopotamians, building a large temple for a god or gods has been a sign of a leader's greatness. Solomon, an Israelite king, built a huge temple to the Hebrew god Yahweh in Jerusalem. Christian kings built magnificent cathedrals in Europe when most people lived in small cottages, and Muslim leaders founded enormous mosques at holy sites across the Near East.

CHAPTER 10

A KING'S HYMN
TO HIMSELF,
"THE WEDDING OF
AMURRU," AND
HAMMURABI'S LAWS

LAYING DOWN THE LAW
HAMMURABI AND THE FIRST LAWMAKERS

Shulgi, "Hymn to Himself," 21st century BCE

King Shulgi was so proud of himself that while other people were writing hymns for the gods, he wrote one to honor himself:

> That my name be established unto distant days and
> that it leave not the mouth of men,
>
> that my praise be spread wide
> in the land, . . .
>
> I, the runner, rose in my
> strength, all set for the course,
>
> and from Nippur to Ur,
> I resolved to travel . . .

Nippur was a city 100 miles north of Ur. Shulgi claimed that he had run these 100 miles, then turned around and run home again—in a huge storm—all in one day. What a sight it must have been to see the king himself running along the soggy dirt roads that bordered the river, pounded by the rain and with mud splashing his legs! Shulgi bragged: "My black-headed people . . . marveled at me." But *did* Shulgi really run two hundred miles in the rain? Or did he make up the story to glorify himself? Actually, he could have written the story himself without a scribe's help. Unlike almost any other Mesopotamian king before

King Shulgi carries a basket of bricks on his head. Though he probably didn't do any building himself, the king commanded that bronze images like this one be placed in the foundations of new temples.

or after him, Shulgi could read and write.

King Shulgi came to the throne in 2094 BCE and Mesopotamia flourished during his 48-year reign. He ruled from Ur during the time known as the Third Dynasty of Ur, or Ur III for short. The Ur III kings, including Shulgi, emphasized the peaceful aspects of their reigns in their inscriptions: they built the first ziggurats (high temple towers for the gods, much taller than the earlier temples on platforms), and they made the roads safe so that people could move between cities without fear of being robbed. Shulgi encouraged trade by setting standards for certain weights and measures. This **standardization** meant that people all over the kingdom could say the same thing and *mean* the same thing.

Under Shulgi, scribes kept track of every tax that was paid, every payment made to a worker, and every donation sent to a temple. We don't know how many clay tablets the scribes filled with these records, but thousands upon thousands have survived.

A U.S. dollar is the same amount of money in Maine and California. And a kilogram is the same in Rome and Beijing. These weights and measurements are standardized—all the same.

Iraqis have partly rebuilt the solid mud-brick ziggurat at Ur with long outside staircases and massive walls. The original upper stories and the small shrine at the top are missing.

Shulgi, Prologue to the Laws, 21st century BCE

Shulgi, Laws, 21st century BCE

"The Wedding of the Amurru," Iraq, 2nd millennium BCE

Even though King Shulgi seems to have had a big ego, he was also concerned about the poor and weak people in his kingdom. He boasted in an inscription "I did not deliver the orphan to the rich. I did not deliver the widow to the mighty...I got rid of hatred [and] violence, and...established justice in the land." In fact, Shulgi put together a list of laws, written on clay tablets. The fragments that survive record the first 37 laws—the earliest written laws the world has ever seen. One of them says that if a man lies in court, "he shall weigh and deliver 15 shekels of silver."

Fifteen shekels was a heavy fine. A later example gives us some idea of exactly how heavy: in 1800 BCE, about three hundred years after Shulgi's reign, a hired laborer earned one shekel of silver for a month's work. So a laborer who was fined 15 shekels would have owed the court his full pay for 450 days, maybe more.

Shulgi's laws named all sorts of crimes: chopping off another man's foot, knocking out someone's tooth, and even cutting off a person's nose. In each law, a punishment was listed for the crime. The fine for breaking a bone was 60 shekels—four times the fine for lying in court. By setting up these strict punishments, Shulgi's laws discouraged people from taking justice into their own hands. If a person was robbed or hurt, he was supposed to go to the judge, explain his case, produce evidence, and then leave the verdict and punishment to the officials.

Like Sargon's empire before it, the Ur III kingdom eventually collapsed, and invaders poured into the country. These invaders were the Amorites, whose name means "westerners," though scholars aren't sure exactly where they came from—only that it was somewhere west of Ur. The Amorites had been a threat during Shulgi's reign, and he had ordered the construction of a long wall to keep them out. But the wall did no good.

When the Amorites arrived, many Mesopotamians thought the end of their civilization had come. One ancient author described an Amorite as a barbarian, "a tent dweller... who eats raw meat; who has no house during the days of his life, and is not buried on the day of his death." But the

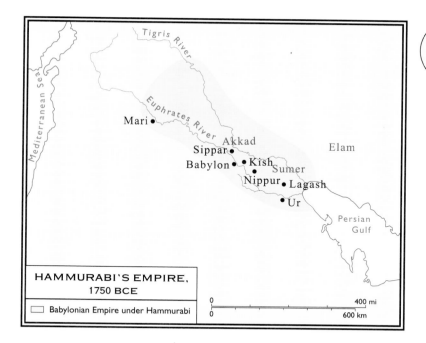

HAMMURABI'S EMPIRE,
1750 BCE

☐ Babylonian Empire under Hammurabi

0   400 mi
0   600 km

Hammurabi was not the
only leader to use the image
of the good shepherd. A
20th century BCE inscrip-
tion from ancient Egypt
describes King Sesostris I in
the same way: "He [the sun
god] appointed me shep-
herd of this land, . . . He
gave to me what he pro-
tects. . . . " Later, according
to the Gospel of John in the
New Testament, Jesus of
Nazareth told his disciples:
"I am the good shepherd.
The good shepherd gives
his life for the sheep."

Amorites didn't bring an end to Mesopotamian prosperity.
Instead they became a part of it. Soon, the newcomers
merged into city life, worshipping the local gods and learning to speak the local language.

One of these Amorite kings, Hammurabi, ruled the city
of Babylon for almost 43 years, from 1792 to 1750 BCE. In
his 29th year on the throne, Hammurabi started building an
empire. Eventually, all of Mesopotamia fell under his control. His empire was the biggest Mesopotamia had seen
since the dynasty of Sargon, almost six hundred years earlier. Like Sargon, Hammurabi claimed he had conquered his
enemies because the gods supported him. He probably
hoped to convince his victims that the gods *wanted* him to
rule over them. Even though his armies must have killed
thousands of people, Hammurabi described himself as the
"shepherd of the people, whose deeds are pleasing to the
goddess Ishtar."

Some of Hammurabi's letters have survived the years,
and documents from other kingdoms of the same period
also refer to him. But most of the records from Hammurabi's

❝ Laws of Hammurabi, around
1755 BCE

reign are lost, probably forever. The water level in the soil at Babylon has risen over the past four thousand years, and water has soaked the buried records. The clay tablets that must have described Hammurabi's accomplishments have turned to mud, and so has the palace itself.

Much of what is known about Hammurabi comes from his laws, which people were still copying down a thousand years after his death. Hammurabi called himself the King of Justice. Somewhat like Shulgi, Hammurabi claimed that he "established justice and freedom in his land." What he meant was that he wiped out everyone's debts. People who had been weighed down with debt were suddenly free to start all over again. Even those who had sold their children or even themselves into slavery were no longer bound. Hammurabi must have become an instant hero to the poor when this decree was announced. (The rich were undoubtedly less pleased.)

Hammurabi, 1792 BCE

With one hand raised in prayer, King Hammurabi stands before Shamash as the god hands him two symbols of his power: a rod and a ring. This carving tops a stone monument that includes Hammurabi's laws.

In his crowning achievement, Hammurabi collected about 282 laws inscribed on a monument that is seven and a half feet high. The laws were written in stone and topped by an image of Hammurabi standing in front of Shamash, the god of justice. In this sculpture, Hammurabi stands in a gesture of prayer, as he receives a rod and a ring—symbols of kingly authority—from Shamash. Even someone who couldn't read would have understood the meaning: Hammurabi had the right to rule and to judge because Shamash had chosen him for these duties.

Hammurabi's laws covered many different kinds of possible court cases: divorce, arguments over property, duties to the king, as well as criminal acts, including theft and assault. Shulgi had punished most crimes with fines. Hammurabi continued to fine people, but added something new. His style of justice sometimes forced the criminal to suffer the same fate as his victim. This type of law is often described as "an eye for an eye." For example, one law states that "If a man should blind the eye of another man, they [the authorities] shall blind his eye."

There's no law against murder in Hammurabi's collection. Perhaps he thought that it was too obvious to be written down. His first law is about an *accusation* of murder: "If a man accuses another man and charges him with murder but cannot bring proof against him, the accuser shall be killed." With such a law in place, no one in his right mind would accuse his enemy of a crime unless he could prove it. The underlying message is this: the court system is powerful and everybody had better respect it—or pay the price.

This bronze figure of a man kneeling in prayer might represent Hammurabi. His face and hands are plated in gold.

Shulgi would have been disappointed. After all his efforts at making a name for himself—running across the country, writing hymns to himself, creating laws—it's Hammurabi who got all the credit. Many textbooks name Hammurabi as the inventor of the world's first laws. But it isn't true. Hammurabi just had the good sense to carve his laws into stone. Most of Shulgi's laws, written in clay, were lost. The few that remain were, for decades, mistakenly credited to Shulgi's father and became known as the Laws of Ur-Nammu.

Poor Shulgi. He tried for glory, but in the long run, he failed.

66 Laws of Hammurabi, around 1755 BCE

66 Laws of Hammurabi, around 1755 BCE

NAME THAT YEAR

In Hammurabi's time, the years had names instead of numbers. Each year, the king chose an event, such as his victory over the Elamites, and named the year for it. The 30th year of Hammurabi's reign became "The year: Hammurabi, the king, the powerful one, beloved of Marduk, by the supreme power of the greatest gods overthrew the army of Elam...he also made firm the foundations of Sumer and Akkad." The next year, he celebrated his victory over the kingdom of Larsa, south of Babylon. These year-names are found on many dated documents. Through them, we can trace the spread of Hammurabi's empire, year by year.

CHAPTER 11

ORDER IN THE COURT!
THE JUSTICE SYSTEM IN MESOPOTAMIA

A Mesopotamian farmer named Ninshubur-tayar lived near the city of Nippur during the reign of Hammurabi, the great lawmaker-king. Ninshubur-tayar owned a house, a field, and an orchard.

After King Hammurabi's death, his son King Samsu-iluna came to the throne. But life on Ninshubur-tayar's farm must have gone on as before, governed by the seasons and the cycles of planting, growing, and harvesting. Ninshubur-tayar's wife, if he ever had one, was no longer alive and he had no living children. Still, he probably ate well. Perhaps he was able to trade his extra crops for a few luxuries—some spices, a wooden chest for his clothes, or a bronze bowl. He seems to have avoided the illnesses and injuries that shortened the lives of so many people of his day.

As Ninshubur-tayar grew old, farm work became more and more difficult for him. He no longer had the energy to work his land the way he once had, but he had no sons who could take over. Hired workmen would be expensive. And what would happen to his farm after he died?

In the 13th year of Samsu-iluna's reign, Ninshubur-tayar adopted a son—not a baby or a little boy. He was too old to raise a child. He needed a strong young man who could farm the land and take care of *him*. The person he chose was Patiya, who may have been a neighbor or a young workman whom Ninshubur-tayar particularly liked.

We can imagine the old man talking to Patiya, explaining his hopes. And we know that Patiya agreed to become Ninshubur-tayar's son because the adoption contract

This legal contract (right) was sealed inside a clay envelope (left), with the text of the contract repeated on the envelope. The inside text could not be changed, so it was the one that counted.

between them has survived. Ninshubur-tayar probably trusted Patiya, but he hired a scribe to draw up a contract—to be on the safe side. The terms of the contract—written in cuneiform script on a rectangular tablet—read:

> Ninshubur-tayar has adopted Patiya as his son. Ninshubur-tayar has given [his] house, field, and orchard to Patiya his son. If Patiya should say to Ninshubur-tayar, . . . "You are not my father," he shall pay one third **mina** of silver. And if Ninshubur-tayar should say to Patiya, . . . "You are not my son," he shall pay one third mina of silver and forfeit his house and possessions. Patiya shall sustain Ninshubur-tayar by a monthly payment of flour and a yearly payment . . . of barley, . . . wool and . . . oil.

❝ Adoption contract, Iraq, 1733 BCE

{ A *mina* weighs approximately one pound.

According to the contract, Patiya would take over Ninshubur-tayar's property and provide his new father with flour for bread, barley for beer, wool for his clothes, and oil for lighting and cooking. The old man would have everything he needed. His new son would care for him for the rest of his life and pray for his soul after he died. Four witnesses, including the scribe, were listed on the contract. The scribe then wrote the date—day, month, and year—and the contract was complete.

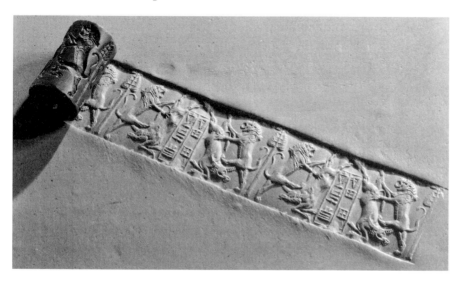

Instead of signing their names on a contract, the witnesses would roll their cylinder seals over the soft clay. Sometimes the text of the contract was written on top of the designs created there.

STICKY FINGERS, BEWARE!

Hammurabi's laws don't include a general rule against stealing. Instead of saying, "You must not steal," as the ancient Hebrew law commands, Hammurabi's laws say, for example, "If a man steals an ox, a sheep, a donkey, a pig, or a boat if it belongs either to the god or the palace, he shall give" 30 times the amount he stole. If the animal or object belonged to a common person, the thief must pay back 10 times the amount. And if the thief "does not have anything to give, he shall be killed."

❝ Adoption contract, Syria, 18th century BCE

Two men face one another over a high table. They have just made a deal between them.

This contract was unusual: if Patiya broke the bargain, his only penalty would be paying a fine. (Usually an adopted son would be sold into slavery if he abandoned his new family.) But if Ninshubur-tayar cancelled the contract, he would not only have to pay a fine, he would also have to give up everything he owned.

Some adoption contracts, especially those that covered the adoption of a young child, included even more protections for the adopted son or daughter. One typical contract from the 18th century BCE, ruled that the adopted child "is the primary heir, and he shall take a double share of the estate of his father. His younger brothers shall divide the remainder in equal shares." This contract decreed that if one of the brothers later went to court over the inheritance, he would have to pay a fine. The terms in this contract gave the adopted son iron-clad protection. No matter how many children eventually joined the family, he would never lose his position and, like all eldest sons in Mesopotamia, would inherit the greatest wealth.

As far as we know, Ninshubur-tayar and Patiya never had any problems. But sometimes adoptions did run into trouble, especially if the parents later had some biological children. Often the children fought over their inheritance after the parents died. When this happened, they usually went to court. Fortunately, the Mesopotamians kept records of some court cases, so we know how their legal system worked.

One of these cases is about a man named Shamash-nasir, whose adoptive father had recently died. Shamash-nasir must have inherited a lot of property or money, and one of his brothers wasn't happy. This brother decided to try his luck in court. According to the record, the brother declared, "Shamash-nasir is not my brother; ... my father did not adopt him." The Mesopotamians had no jury system, so a panel of six or seven judges had to decide whether or not the adoption had been legal. The Mesopotamians had no lawyers either, so Shamash-nasir defended himself. When one of the judges asked for his statement, "Shamash-nasir answered him, saying: 'Awil-Nabium, my father, while I was a small child, took me in adoption and reared me, I can produce witnesses ...' thus he spoke."

Just as in court cases today, the judges called for witnesses and "then listened carefully to their testimony." They "sent them to the temple of Shamash in order to declare their testimony under oath" in the presence of the gods. The witnesses swore that Shamash-nasir had been adopted legally, and their evidence closed the case. The jealous brother didn't seem to have any witnesses, so he lost the case *and* his share of papa's money.

Contracts weren't just for adoptions. The Mesopotamians also used them for sales and rentals of houses and fields, marriages, purchases of slaves, even the hire of workmen. And always, at the end, came a list of witnesses. Without witnesses, a Mesopotamian contract wasn't worth the clay it was written on. The judges in a court case often consulted the contracts, if there were any. And they also would have considered the laws proclaimed by the king.

Hammurabi's laws aren't general rules. They never say that people should "never" or "always" do something. Instead, they cover particular situations—if *this*, then *that*. So the written laws don't cover even a fraction of the possible cases that might wind up in court. They couldn't have, and no one knows how carefully the judges tried to follow them. Did they use the written laws as their guides or did they act on their best *judgment*? Probably both.

Inheritance claim, Iraq, 18th to 17th century BCE

LIAR, LIAR, PANTS ON FIRE!

A witness could make or break a Mesopotamian court case. Everyone knew that lying under oath brought a huge fine. And a witness who lied in a murder case could be put to death. Lying was especially scary because if the judge didn't catch the dishonest witness, the gods would. Like witnesses in modern courtrooms who swear "to tell the truth and nothing but the truth," ancient witnesses promised to tell the truth in the presence of Shamash, the all-seeing god of the sun. The Mesopotamians believed that Shamash especially hated lying and might strike a person dead on the spot for swearing falsely in his name. No wonder the Mesopotamians took their oaths so seriously!

CHAPTER 12

FARMERS AND DOCTORS, BARBERS AND BUILDERS

MESOPOTAMIAN WORKERS, SLAVE AND FREE

CLAY, CLAY, GLOOO-RIOUS CLAY!

The ancient Greeks, Romans, and Egyptians wrote on papyrus—a type of paper made from reeds—whereas the Mesopotamians wrote on clay tablets. Papyrus may seem to be more modern, but papyrus can be torn or burned, and, in time, falls apart. Although some papyrus texts have survived, especially in the dry Egyptian desert, most disintegrated. The Greek and Roman histories, myths, and other works that have come down to us are copies of copies.

Sunbaked clay lasts almost forever. And this is why we still have many original Mesopotamian texts—not just copies. The clay tablets that Mesopotamian scribes wrote on tell us about the lives of people who lived, worked, and died thousands of years ago. The surprising thing is that the Mesopotamian texts sometimes tell us more about the lives of *ordinary* people—such as gardeners, weavers, and merchants—than about the lives of the kings, queens, and priests who ruled over them.

Ningallam was one such ordinary person. She was a slave, but we know her name because scribes wrote it, month after month, in the records of the palace where they all worked. There are several ways that Ningallam might have become a slave. For example, she might have been a prisoner of war, or she might have been born to slave parents and purchased by the queen's palace.

Ningallam raised pigs for the queen's palace in the Sumerian city of Lagash around 2400 BCE. The ancient records tell us that Ningallam received 18 liters of barley each month—which equals 4¾ gallons. Her two children must have helped their mother in her work, because they too received monthly rations of grain. Poor children could not go to school. Instead, they learned their parents' crafts and began working at an early age.

Together, Ningallam's family received 42 liters of grain a month—barely enough to survive on. Many modern families buy milk in plastic jugs. The largest size holds a gallon. Imagine 10½ of these filled with grain. That's how much Ningallam and her children received each month. But later the pattern changed and, for a while, Ningallam's name

Women spun, dyed, and wove fabric for their families—and sometimes for priests and the royal family too.

appeared without her usual rations. Her children's names were still listed as receiving their usual 12 liters each. Why was Ningallam left out? A later text gives the answer; it lists the "children of Ningallam" as "orphans." Ningallam had died. But her name was still on the lists. Why? Perhaps it was to identify who her children were, because this was before the invention of last names.

Not much is known about how slaves were treated in ancient Mesopotamia. But we do know that Ningallam's children kept on raising pigs for the palace because her children's names appear in palace records for many years.

Thousands of people worked for the temples and palaces. Some, like Ningallam and her children, raised animals. Others wove cloth, made tools and weapons, created fine jewelry, or brewed beer. Still others made furniture, carved stone statues and inscriptions, or tanned leather. Some worked in teams in or near the palace and temple buildings, but others worked outside the town limits. Ningallam's pigs probably weren't kept anywhere near the palace—too smelly. Metalworkers also worked in the

" Records from a queen's estate, Iraq, 2400 BCE

countryside because the very hot fires that they used made a lot of smoke. But the palace and temples paid them all with grain, oil, and wool, and the scribes wrote their names on clay tablets.

Some workers were better paid than Ningallam was, and most weren't slaves. Some workers received more grain, oil, and wool than they actually needed for survival. These lucky ones had enough left over to buy other things that they wanted. Some were even paid in silver. Workers usually expected to receive one shekel or less of silver a month. Even though a shekel only weighed about eight grams (about the weight of two squares from a chocolate bar), it went pretty far. One collection of laws from around 1900 BCE lists what a shekel of silver could buy:

66 Laws of Eshnunna, Iraq, 1900 BCE

- 79 gallons of barley, or
- ¾ gallon of best oil, or
- ⅖ gallon of pig's fat, or
- 6 pounds of wool, or
- 158 gallons of salt, or
- 3 pounds of copper

Many families would have spent most of their income on food. A family of three would need about fifty liters of

Mesopotamian temples kept sets of weights ranging from the large mina to the much tinier shekel.

barley a month. Ningallam's family received much less. They would also have needed salt for seasoning, wool for clothing, and oil for cooking and lighting. (People in the ancient Near East used oil lamps to light their homes at night.) They probably grew vegetables in a small garden and added to their diet with fish from the river. A worker who received more barley than he or she needed each month could trade some of it for other goods.

Top palace and temple officials were paid in land that they could farm. With the help of hired workers, they could become rich from the sale of their farm products. By the time of Hammurabi's empire, more people owned their own farms and had started businesses than in Ningallam's time.

If you could walk through a Mesopotamian city in Hammurabi's time, the sights and smells would tell you a lot about the types of work that went on and the lives of the workers there.

On one street you might find bakers, sweating in the summer heat as their ovens baked loaves of bread. Farther along a potter might have his kilns going, firing a batch of clay bowls and jars that he would sell later. The neighborhood handyman might be melting down metal scraps, planning to reshape them later into things his neighbors might buy. Imagine the mingled aromas of bread, smoke, and hot metal.

Further along, you might find a tavern, at the corner of two streets. Taverns, which were often owned by women, weren't always very respectable because criminals often hung out there. Hammurabi mentioned this problem in his law 109: "If there should be a woman innkeeper in whose house criminals gather, and she fails to . . . lead them off to the palace authorities, that woman innkeeper shall be killed."

Professionals—important people such as physicians, veterinarians, builders, and barbers—also lived and worked in the city. The king's barber was often one of the king's closest advisors. (Anyone who regularly held a sharp knife that near the king's head had better be trustworthy!) But even the barber had to follow certain rules—or get into trouble. He wasn't allowed to cut a slave's hair in such a way

PAYING THE BILL

The Mesopotamians invented a clever way of paying for things before coins were invented. A wealthy man would wear a coil of silver around his wrist. When he wanted to buy something, he would just snip off a bit of silver, which would be weighed on a scale. Although each merchant probably kept a set of weights, the only ones that everyone accepted as accurate were the ones in the temple. If a merchant tried to cheat his customers by using false weights, his set could be checked against the temple set. The first coins in the world were invented in Lydia (in modern Turkey) in the sixth century BCE. This invention made shopping much easier!

❝ Laws of Hammurabi, around 1755 BCE

❝ Laws of Hammurabi, around 1755 BCE

that the hairstyle no longer identified him or her as a slave. One of Hammurabi's laws said that "If a barber shaves off the slave-hairlock . . . without the slave owner's permission, they shall cut off that barber's hand."

Some of the biggest houses you would see, on this walk through the city, would belong to the merchants who brought luxury materials from other lands. Few of the merchants traveled personally. They usually hired trading agents who did the hard, and often dangerous, work of traveling to foreign places.

Now that towns were becoming more prosperous and traders were bringing luxury goods to Mesopotamia, where did ordinary Mesopotamians do their shopping? If they were farmers, their farms produced much of what they needed to eat and most families seem to have woven their own cloth from the wool of their sheep. (Even people who made a living in another way, such as innkeepers and priests, often owned farmland as well.) But they still must have needed to buy pots, tools, and furniture. They may have had surplus grain or vegetables to sell, as well. There were public squares in the cities, and people also seem to have gathered at open spaces near the city gates. They may have set up their markets in these places, like ancient shopping centers—the Southgate Mall, perhaps?

A Mesopotamian shopkeeper holds the scales that he uses to weigh metals. If customers didn't trust him, the merchant's scales could be checked against the "master set" in the temple.

CHAPTER 13

UR-UTU'S STORY
THE MESOPOTAMIAN FAMILY

Ur-Utu hadn't seen the disaster coming. Now foreign tribes were attacking the city. Panic flew through the streets of Sippar. Everyone had to pack up and get out of town. Even though he was a wealthy man and a priest, Ur-Utu had no protection against the invaders. He must have alerted his relatives while his servants wrapped the family's treasures in rugs or cloth bags, ready to run. But before Ur-Utu abandoned his home, he rushed into his study where thousands of written records were kept. How frantic he must have been when he realized how little he could take with him!

Over the years, Ur-Utu had kept letters, contracts for the sale of houses and fields, loan agreements, lists, prayers, and even old school exercise tablets. He probably wanted to take them all, but they were written on clay tablets, most of which were about half an inch thick and about the size of a grown man's hand—too heavy and bulky for him to carry them all. Ur-Utu had to choose.

Because he could read, Ur-Utu was able to glance at each document and quickly decide if it was important enough to save. He tossed many on the floor and picked 49 to take with him. Most were records that proved his ownership of large fields, the main source of his family's wealth. In addition to these **receipts**, he also chose some loan contracts showing who owed him silver and barley.

Now Ur-Utu *really* had to leave. Probably his house was already on fire. Imagine him choking and coughing as the smoke and flames spread, gathering the chosen documents in his arms...stumbling toward the door. And then disaster struck. In his haste, Ur-Utu tripped on two steps between rooms, and the tablets fell to the floor. Ur-Utu gave up. He left the documents where they lay and ran for his life.

The story of Ur-Utu's escape is not a made-up scene from a Hollywood script. Twentieth-century archaeologists pieced it together when they excavated the Mesopotamian

People today keep the deed when they buy a house and save the receipts from big purchases, such as laptop computers. These documents are a lot like Mesopotamian records, except that ours are not written on clay.

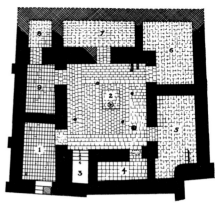

The rooms in ancient Near Eastern houses opened onto a central courtyard (number 2 in this drawing by archaeologist Leonard Woolley). A windowless wall faced the street to protect the family's privacy and to guard against outside noise and smells.

THE LONGEST NAMES

Mesopotamian names were actually phrases or sentences. Inanna-mansum's name, for instance, meant, "Inanna [goddess of love] has given [this child]." Shulgi meant, "noble young man" and Hammurabi meant, "[the god] Hammu is great" or perhaps "[the god] Hammu heals." Two sons of King Sargon the Great must have been twins because the second one's name meant, "Who is with him?" Perhaps that's what his mother said, in surprise, when the second baby was born. A girl's name might include the name of a god's wife, such as Shamash's wife Aya—"Gift-from-Aya," for example. Many names could be used for either boys or girls.

city of Sippar. They found that the whole city was abandoned after foreign invaders attacked around 1650 BCE. No one ever lived in Ur-Utu's house after he left it, and no one ever came back for the documents. No bones were found, so everyone must have gotten out safely. Ur-Utu's treasured records remained untouched—covered by the broken walls of his house—for thousands of years, until archaeologists began to investigate.

They discovered evidence that the house had been burned. The priest's study was a mess, with records tossed on the floor. They found the most important documents right where Ur-Utu abandoned them: on the floor of a room at the top of two steps.

To find so much about one man and his family is rare, but Ur-Utu's house even had records from his parents' time. From them, we're able to get a glimpse of family life in ancient Mesopotamia. Ur-Utu's father, who also served as a priest, was named Inanna-mansum, and it is his life that the documents tell us most about.

After his parents died, Inanna-mansum came into his inheritance and decided to choose a wife. Marriage in Mesopotamia was an arrangement between families, not a romantic relationship. A man might have met the girl he wanted to marry, but the two of them wouldn't have gone places together. That would have caused a scandal. So when Inanna-mansum chose a young woman named Ilsha-hegalli, he would have visited her father and asked permission to marry her. If the father agreed, the two men would have sat down together to work out an arrangement. We don't know whether Ilsha-hegalli had a choice or not. Like most Mesopotamian brides, she was probably still a teenager.

Ilsha-hegalli's dad would have wanted to know if Inanna-mansum could support his daughter. And what gift, he would have asked, had Inanna-mansum brought to show that he was serious about his offer of marriage? Inanna-mansum would have asked about the bride's dowry—what wealth would she bring to the marriage? This could be furniture, household goods, land, livestock, or other valuables.

Ilsha-hegalli's dowry was probably similar to one that was described in a document found in Ur-Utu's house. This dowry included:

- 1 slave girl
- 1 bed
- 5 chairs
- 1 . . . grindstone of black basalt [for grinding grain] . . .
- copper cauldrons . . .
- chests . . . [and]
- a splendid garment

66 Dowry list, Iraq, 17th century BCE

Each of these things was expensive. The furnishings were handmade from imported materials, such as fine wood, copper, and basalt.

A Mesopotamian woman's dowry was actually her inheritance, and it came to her when she married. Her brothers had to wait for their share of the property until the deaths of their parents. A woman's dowry remained her property until she passed it on to her children. A husband could *use* the dowry property. For instance, he could sleep in the bed and sit on the chairs, but the furniture belonged to the wife. In order for a marriage to be

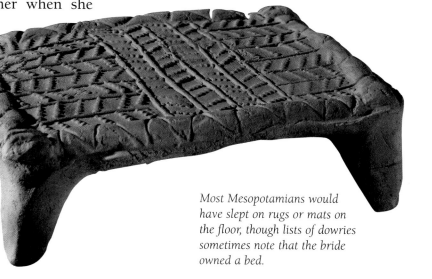

Most Mesopotamians would have slept on rugs or mats on the floor, though lists of dowries sometimes note that the bride owned a bed.

“ Laws of Hammurabi, around
1755 BCE

“ Marriage contract, Iraq, 17th
century BCE

legal, there had to be a contract. Hammurabi's law 128 says: "If a man marries a wife but does not draw up a formal contract for her, that woman is not a wife." In other words, a marriage wasn't legal without a contract. Often the terms of divorce were written right into the marriage document. One contract, written during Ur-Utu's lifetime, decreed: "If [the groom] says to [the bride], . . . 'You are not my wife,' he must pay half a pound of silver. If [the bride] says to her husband . . . 'You are not my husband,' they [the authorities] shall tie her up and throw her into the water." Half a pound of silver was 30 shekels—more than two years' salary for a worker. But this was nothing compared to the woman's punishment: she would be killed!

Not all marriage contracts favored the husband this much. Occasionally, a wife could get a divorce by paying her husband a certain amount of silver. Hammurabi's laws made an exception for a good woman who was married to a cruel, wandering husband or one who said bad things about her. Such a woman could take her dowry and go back to her father's house.

After the marriage ceremony, the new bride moved into her husband's home. Often the groom's parents still lived in the same house, and perhaps a brother and his family did, too. Sometimes family members—brothers, uncles, cousins—filled up a whole city block, living in neighboring or connected homes.

A married woman stayed in touch with her parents, brothers, and sisters. She was expected to help them out if they were having trouble of some kind. This was probably true of Ilsha-hegalli, because she had married into a wealthy family. Most likely, she sent gifts to her brothers and sisters as a sign of her love for them. One woman wrote a complaining letter to her married

This board game, found in a royal tomb, looks a lot like checkers—and it was. Players moved the round counters around the squares. (You wouldn't want the dead person to get bored, would you?)

sister: "Send me one hundred locusts and food worth one-sixth of a shekel of silver. In this, I will see your sisterly feelings toward me." Locusts—crunchy insects with wings, related to grasshoppers—were considered to be an especially tasty treat.

The house into which Ilsha-hegalli moved with Inanna-mansum was the same house that later burned down. Visitors would have entered the quiet of the house through a wooden door that led into a central courtyard. In summer, the air was hot and still in the courtyard, even in the shade. There, Ilsha-hegalli would have kept her loom for making the family's clothes. The brick oven where she cooked bread was in the courtyard, too.

Doorways opened from the courtyard to the other rooms, which were relatively cool inside because of the thick, mud-brick walls. These rooms did not have much furniture. Most Meso-potamian houses were decorated with rugs, cushions, and wall hangings, rather than tables and chairs. One room of the house was tiled with baked bricks and probably served as a bathroom. The water would have been brought in from outdoor wells in pottery tubs.

When their family began to grow, Ilsha-hegalli and Inanna-mansum would have worried when their children became ill. Many infants and toddlers died from diseases that are no longer dangerous today. These deaths must have been heartbreaking, and Mesopotamian parents tried to protect their children with chants, prayers, and magical charms that the children wore around their necks. Mothers sang lullabies to try to keep their little ones from crying,

❝ Letter, Iraq, 19th to 16th century BCE

When archaeologists excavated Ur-Utu's house, they found the bottoms of walls of the rooms. They figured out how each room had been used by studying the objects found inside.

ATTACK OF THE KILLER BOO-BOOS

Fifty was old in ancient Mesopotamia. A simple cut or a tooth abscess could become infected and cause death in those days. Childbirth took the lives of many young women, and war ended the lives of many men. There were no vaccines against childhood diseases, and terrible epidemics killed thousands. Still, a few people lived to be old. Hammurabi reigned for 43 years, so he must have been at least 60 when he died. And very, very occasionally, people lived into their 80s or 90s. Someone that old might have been tempted to exaggerate his or her age. After all, there were no birth certificates then—and few others could remember the person's birth. Perhaps this is where the myths came from of people in ancient times living to be hundreds of years old.

because they believed that loud noises made the gods angry.

Unfortunately, the Mesopotamian scribes don't tell us much about childhood. We can guess that, when they were young, Ur-Utu and his brothers and sisters played with toys, such as the balls and clay wagons that archaeologists have found in the tells. Later, Ur-Utu went to a scribal school so that he could follow in his father's footsteps, serving as a priest. Less privileged boys would have learned from their fathers how to manage a farm or a business. Mesopotamian mothers taught their daughters how to grind grain, cook, wash, spin wool, weave cloth, and take care of children.

Few women held jobs outside the home in ancient Mesopotamia, probably because they married as teenagers and usually had big families. Managing the household was a full-time job. But women had more rights than in many other ancient cultures. Unlike Greek women, for example, Mesopotamian women could go out in public, and could even own businesses, such as taverns. Women from wealthy families could become priestesses and could own and control fields and orchards.

When Ur-Utu grew to manhood, he married a woman named Ra'imtum, and she came to live in the house with her husband, his parents, his sister, and one of his brothers. Over time, Ur-Utu, as a landowner, became one of the richest men in the city. But then the invaders came. . . . We don't know what happened to Ur-Utu. After his city was abandoned, he may have moved to another town. Did he make a new start somewhere else? Did he live to be old—old enough to tell his grandchildren the story of his dramatic escape?

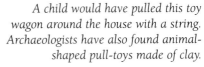

A child would have pulled this toy wagon around the house with a string. Archaeologists have also found animal-shaped pull-toys made of clay.

CHAPTER 14

SCRIBES, SCHOOL, AND SCHOOLBOYS

EDUCATION IN ANCIENT MESOPOTAMIA

❝ SUMERIAN STORIES, A CONTRACT, AND A RIDDLE

I got up early in the morning. I turned to my mother and said: "Give me my lunch. I want to go to school." My mother gave me two rolls, and I set out. . . . In the school, the man in charge of punctuality demanded, "Why are you late?" Afraid and with a pounding heart, I went to my teacher and made a respectful bow.

❝ "Schooldays," Iraq, around 2000 BCE

The student who wrote these words tried to show proper respect to his teacher, but it did him no good. The headmaster immediately found a mistake in his work and caned him—whacked him with a long stick. Next he was caned for hanging around in the street and for being sloppily dressed. Before the day was done, the boy had been caned nine times, once for messy handwriting and later for talking during class. He was punished for speaking in his native language of Akkadian rather than Sumerian, the official language of the school. He stood up when he shouldn't have and later left the building without permission. The poor guy couldn't do anything right that day! So many people seemed to be watching and waiting for him to make a mistake—not just teachers and the headmaster (the "school father"). Older students, called "big brothers," also disciplined the younger students and made them behave.

Who was this boy? In many ways, he sounds like a modern student on a *really* bad day. But he wasn't. He lived in ancient Sumer around 2000 BCE, and when he grew up, he became a scribe. This story became a school exercise for

Schoolchildren learned to write by copying lines of cuneiform. The teacher wrote the first and third lines on this tablet, and a student wrote on the second and fourth lines.

students to copy, and archaeologists have found lots of copies among the thousands of tablets that have survived from these ancient times. Was it used as a warning or did teachers and students laugh about the kid who kept messing up?

Only wealthy parents could afford to send their children to the scribal schools in Mesopotamia. (*Scribe* literally means "one who writes.") Reading and writing prepared students to become well-paid professionals: scribes, doctors, judges, priests, and astronomers.

A scribe (third from right) holds a tablet in his left hand and a stylus in his right. He may have just been summoned by the king to take dictation.

Almost all the students were boys. In the thousands of years of Mesopotamia's history, a few women became scribes, but not many. Most women worked at home and were not expected to have professions. The few female scribes that we know of generally worked for other women: queens, princesses, and priestesses. Historians don't know if they went to the scribal schools with the boys or if they were trained by older women scribes. We know nothing about these women except their names.

Clay tablets—student workbooks—have told us a lot about the lives of the male students. Some were the sons and grandsons of scribes; others were the sons of kings, officials, and merchants. But not all wealthy parents sent their sons to school. Most of them saw no need to learn to read and write. Why bother when they could afford to hire scribes to do these things *for* them? So only a tiny percentage of the population went to school. Most boys, especially the poor ones, had no choice but to spend their days working in the fields with their brothers or learning the trades of their fathers.

Almost everything that happened in the scribal schools involved tablets. In fact, the school itself was called an *edubba* or "tablet house." All day, every day—except for a lunch break—the students used their clay tablets. They spent long hours on vocabulary, learning to recognize and write the cuneiform signs that were used in writing the Sumerian and Akkadian languages. Most people spoke Akkadian in their everyday lives. But boys in scribal schools learned to speak and write Sumerian because it was the official language for contracts, letters, and temple documents—and because it was used in the temples to speak to the gods.

Boys probably started school when they were quite young and finished in their late teens. Their studies must have been pretty boring, by modern standards. There were no sports, arts, or crafts to break up the day, and no classes in history or science either. The students learned language, literature, mathematics, and music, almost all through memorization.

When they were first learning to write, students copied simple lines of cuneiform that the teacher had written out. Later on, they copied popular myths and legends, and their copies are our best sources for the stories that had been passed down for many generations. In language study, the boys memorized lists of Sumerian words with the Akkadian words that meant the same thing. They recited the words, then practiced writing them. The lists weren't in alphabetical order, but in groups—names of animals, foods, or body parts, for example.

The students sat on brick benches as they wrote on round tablets of soft clay with a stylus, a pointed writing tool made from a reed. Their strict teachers ordered harsh punishments, but the rewards of education were great. A boy who studied hard could become an important, respected

MATHEMATICS, MESOPOTAMIAN STYLE

Mesopotamian mathematics was based on 60, instead of 10, as ours is. In some ways, it makes sense because 60 can be divided by 2, 3, 4, 5, 6, 10, and 12, and the Mesopotamians used a lot of fractions. (Ten can only be divided by 2 and 5.) Students, then as now, used mathematical tables to help them with multiplication, square roots, and exponents. The remains of Mesopotamian math are hiding in our modern clocks and calendars. Our 60-second minute, 60-minute hour, and 360-degree circle are all legacies from ancient Mesopotamia. The Mesopotamians also gave us the idea of place notation when we write numbers: putting ones in one column, tens in another column, hundreds in another, and so on.

Mesopotamian mathematicians could calculate area, even of irregular shapes like the one plotted on this tablet from 2100 BCE. When a field was sold, the contract often listed its area.

"The Disputation between Enkimansi and Girnishag," Iraq, around 2000 BCE

Royal land gift contract, Syria, around 1650 BCE

Riddle, Iraq, date unknown

man like Pagirum, a scribe who lived around 1650 BCE. Pagirum was self-employed. He earned a living by writing letters or contracts for people who couldn't read or write for themselves. He knew how to use proper legal language and could take dictation, quickly writing down another person's words as he spoke. He understood enough mathematics to survey houses and fields to calculate their sizes when they were about to be sold or divided among family members.

Not all scribes were equally good at their duties. In an ancient text that was often copied by schoolboys, one scribe made fun of another scribe: "When you write a document, it makes no sense. When you write a letter, it's unreadable. You try to divide up an estate, but you can't do it . . . you can't even hold the measuring line. . . . You don't know how to work with arguing clients, and you make the trouble worse between quarreling brothers."

Although most of Pagirum's clients were ordinary citizens, he probably worked for the king occasionally, too. After many years in his profession—perhaps Pagirum was an old man by then—the local king rewarded him, "Ammimadar, the king . . . gave these fields to Pagirum, his servant." With this gift of 51 acres, he could grow food to support his family. A different scribe drew up this contract, listing the fields, their sizes, locations, and borders. He wrote that if anyone else tried to claim Pagirum's land, he would owe "ten pounds of silver to the palace, and hot asphalt will be smeared on his head."

Pagirum had benefited all his life from his schooling, just as a Mesopotamian riddle said he would: "He whose eyes are not open enters it. He whose eyes are wide open comes out of it." What is it?

"School."

CHAPTER 15

LOVERS, SISTERS, AND COOKS

SCENES FROM A MESOPOTAMIAN PALACE

To my lord, a letter from Shibtu, your servant. All is well at the palace. All is well, too, with the temples of the gods and the workshops. I have had omens read for the health of my lord. These omens are good... but my lord must take good care of himself when he is in the full sun.

❝ Shibtu, letter to Zimri-Lim, 18th century BCE

Shibtu dictated this letter to a scribe and sent it by messenger to her "lord," King Zimri-Lim of Mari. In it, she called herself a servant. But this was just a way of showing respect. Shibtu was not a hired servant. She was, instead, a very powerful woman: the king's chief **wife**. As a king's daughter herself, she had lived in palaces all her life and knew what was required of a queen.

Shibtu was very fond of her husband. When he was out fighting, she worried about him and often wrote, begging him to take care of himself. She warned him against staying too long in the sizzling desert sun, knowing that people could collapse—even die—from heat exhaustion and dehydration.

Zimri-Lim also sent letters home to Shibtu, often telling her about his military campaigns. But sometimes, he was unable to write right away, and then Shibtu would worry. Had he been injured... or killed? It must have been hard for her to wait for messengers

In Mesopotamia, kings often had more than one wife, which increased the odds of having an heir to follow them on the throne, but other men could marry only one woman at a time.

Too bad this royal lady from Mari has lost her head, but at least her tasseled shawl and elegant necklace remain. Her long hair, visible in the back of the statue, is braided.

BUBBLE, BUBBLE, TOIL, AND...BEER

The people of Mari, like all Mesopotamians, drank beer more than any other beverage. And they were the first to brew it. They made their beer from barley and water, using natural yeast to ferment the mixture. (Yeast is a tiny fungus found in the air—the same organism that causes bread dough to rise.) Fermentation not only made the brew bubbly, but it also served to kill the bacteria that were often found in the water.

to bring his letters. Once she wrote "My heart has been greatly alarmed. . . . May a tablet come from my lord so that my heart may be calmed."

When Zimri-Lim was away from the palace, Shibtu handled the day-to-day running of the palace and the kingdom. Even when the king was at home, she managed the royal household. Her large staff included weavers, leather workers, stonemasons, jewelers, woodworkers, goldsmiths, bronze workers, gardeners, water carriers, basket weavers, cooks, and scribes. These workers included some prisoners of war as well as local people who had been trained in various crafts. All of them were paid in rations of bread, oil, and wool.

French archaeologists have found more than 20,000 cuneiform tablets in the palace at Mari, an ancient Syrian city on the Euphrates in ancient times. Many of them were written during the reign of Zimri-Lim, who lived at the same time as King Hammurabi of Babylon. The tablets from Mari, which include the short messages between Zimri-Lim and Shibtu, give us the clearest picture we have of royal life in Mesopotamia in the beginning of the 18th century BCE.

Like Hammurabi, Zimri-Lim was a warrior, judge, diplomat, religious leader, and devoted king to his people.

MESOPOTAMIA AND HATTI, 1800–1600 BCE

Although Hammurabi's personal life remains a mystery, we know quite a lot about Zimri-Lim. He had 11 daughters, maybe more. He had one son also, but the boy died young. At least nine of the daughters married the rulers of nearby lands. The girls had no say in choosing their husbands. Their marriages were designed to cement friendships between the king and his allies—insurance policies against war and rebellion. Love, if it bloomed, was a bonus, but often that didn't happen.

One of Zimri-Lim's daughters, Inib-sharri, was desperately unhappy in her marriage. Her husband, a king, already had a wife before he married Inib-sharri. The two women didn't get along, and Inib-sharri wrote to her father that the other wife had forced her "to sit in the corner, and caused me, like an idiot, to hold my cheek in my hand." Inib-sharri wrote that the king made it clear that he liked the other wife more: "His eating and drinking is continuous before this woman, [while I could not] open my mouth.... What about me?"

Inib-sharri's complaints eventually convinced Zimri-Lim that the situation was impossible. He wrote to his daughter: "Gather your household [servants and belongings]. If that's not possible, just cover your head and leave."

When another daughter, Shimatum, married, Zimri-Lim gave her a generous dowry, including fine furniture, fancy clothes, jewelry, and 10 maidservants to attend her every need. But things did not go well in the first years of Shimatum's marriage to King Haya-Sumu. Perhaps she was unable to give him an heir—the records don't say—but, after three years, Zimri-Lim sent Shimatum's sister Kirum to the same kingdom as a second wife for Haya-Sumu. Instead of sticking together, the sisters became rivals. Both women wrote to their father, and each one tried to convince him that *she* was the one who deserved his support.

The letters from Shimatum and Kirum have opened a window onto an ancient case of sibling rivalry. Kirum should have held the lesser position in court, because Shimatum was the king's first wife. But Kirum didn't see it that way. She wanted the place of honor. Shimatum tattled

📖 Inib-sharri, letter to Zimri-Lim, 18th century BCE

📖 Zimri-Lim, letter to Inib-sharri, 18th century BCE

"" Shimatum, letter to Zimri-Lim, 18th century BCE

"" Kirum, letter to Zimri-Lim, 18th century BCE

to papa, painting herself as Kirum's innocent victim: "There is neither fault nor crime on my part."

Luckily for Shimatum, the King Haya-Sumu didn't like his pushy second wife and treated her badly in front of guests. So then Kirum wrote to papa:

> Haya-Sumu rose up against me and said, "Are you acting as the boss here?" . . . Then he took away from me my very last maidservants. May my father send me just one . . . reliable man among his servants, so that I can come home quickly? . . . If my lord does not . . . bring me home, I shall surely die.

When King Haya-Sumu finally divorced Kirum, Shimatum had no sympathy for her once-proud sister, even though Kirum had threatened to throw herself from the highest rooftop. The records suggest that Zimri-Lim *did* send for Kirum, and the battle between the sisters ended.

The letters from Zimri-Lim's many daughters show that they stayed in touch with their parents and siblings after their marriages. They sent and received gifts, and they kept their father up-to-date on politics in their adopted lands. Zimri-Lim received letters from his advisors and various palace officials, too. Governors of the cities within the kingdom also wrote to the king, as did his ambassadors to foreign courts. Many of the letters written to Zimri-Lim have survived.

The palace at Mari was enormous in Zimri-Lim's time. Covering about six acres, it had more than 260 rooms on the ground floor alone. Much of the palace was given over to official business, but the king and his family had their private quarters, where guards protected their safety and privacy.

When an ambassador first arrived at Zimri-Lim's court, servants would have filled the bathtub in the palace bathroom so that the ambassador could enjoy a nice soak after his travels. This bathroom even had a "flush toilet" perched over a running stream that washed away the

This bronze lion protected Dagan's temple at Mari. Wild lions roamed Syria in the 18th century BCE. When one was captured, the hunter would send it to King Zimri-Lim so that he could hunt it on his royal estate.

In this palace wall painting, the king of Mari, wearing a white robe and tall hat, receives the symbols of power—the ring and the rod—from a goddess. Goddesses and fantastic animals watch among tall palms.

waste. Refreshed and tidied up, the ambassador would have been escorted through a small door on the far right side of the large courtyard into a dark, L-shaped corridor. The sunlight streaming through a door in the corridor would have lit his way into the king's own court. Here, the visiting ambassador would wait in the shade of tall potted palm trees until Zimri-Lim was ready to receive him in his throne room.

One wall in the throne room was decorated with a large painting that depicted a king dressed in elegant robes, receiving the symbols of authority (the rod and ring) from a goddess. The other walls were probably hung with tapestries and rich carpets probably covered the floor. When the ambassador was finally admitted to the king's presence, Zimri-Lim would have been seated upon an elaborate throne made from ivory and gold.

ONE OF THE WORLD'S OLDEST RECIPES

This ancient Mesopotamian recipe tells how to cook Kippu-Bird in Mint Sauce. The birds "are first split open, rinsed in cold water... [and] placed in a kettle," where they are quickly seared. The instructions continue: remove the kettle from the heat and add "a little cold water... and a sprinkling of vinegar. Then mint and salt are pounded together and rubbed into the kippu, after which the liquid... is strained and mint is added to this sauce." The bird is then put back into the kettle. When all the ingredients have blended, the dish is complete.

After seeing the king, perhaps the ambassador would have been invited to visit Zimri-Lim's temple or to see the archive rooms where the palace records were stored. And then that night, the king would have honored him and his assistants with a feast. Cooks and kitchen servants would have worked all day, scurrying back and forth between the storage rooms, the kitchens, and the dining hall.

A high-ranking woman named Ama-dugga controlled all the food in Zimri-Lim's palace. She commanded a large staff of men and women who brewed beer, ground flour, made cakes and pastries, then cooked and served the meals. Excavations from other Mesopotamian sites have even provided us with recipes written on clay tablets—the earliest known recipes in the world. These recipes, mostly for meat and bread dishes, feature herbs (such as mint), spices (such as cumin), plus lots of onions, garlic, and leeks. Unlike the average person, Zimri-Lim probably ate meat every day. And what did Ama-dugga keep in the pantry for royal desserts? Dates—the Mesopotamians' favorite fruit.

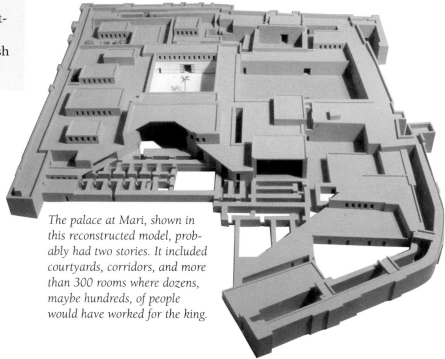

The palace at Mari, shown in this reconstructed model, probably had two stories. It included courtyards, corridors, and more than 300 rooms where dozens, maybe hundreds, of people would have worked for the king.

CHAPTER 16

THE SURPRISE ENDING OF THE BABYLONIAN EMPIRE

HITTITE VICTORIES AND INDO-EUROPEAN LANGUAGES

The king of Babylon Samsu-ditana must have felt pretty smug and secure. Though the empire had shrunk during the 140 years since Great-Great-Great Grandfather Hammurabi sat on the throne, Babylon was still *the* major power in the ancient Near East. By the beginning of the 16th century BCE, the kingdom of Babylon had not been attacked for centuries.

Then, in 1595 BCE, the scribal records suddenly stop and, for generations, there's no news of Babylon or its king. Hammurabi's descendants never again ruled Babylon. Something terrible must have happened. But what?

In most situations, archaeologists could dig up some answers by excavating the site, but that's impossible for Babylon. The water in the soil has risen, completely soaking the earth at the level where the ancient city lies buried. The answer turned to mud!

Whatever happened in Babylon was sudden and a complete surprise. The city was demolished, though many people survived. Some of them told the story to their descendants. Many years later, a Mesopotamian writer mentioned the disaster of 1595 BCE: "In the time of Samsu-ditana, the Man of Hatti marched against Akkad." Finally, a clue!

Akkad was the old name for the kingdom of Babylon, but who was this "Man of Hatti"? Archaeologists found the answer, not in Babylon itself but hundreds of miles north,

Storage rooms and workrooms surrounded this temple, set in the hilly countryside of Anatolia. In the center was a courtyard. Excavations at Hattusa have uncovered many temples and palaces built of stone.

'' Babylonian Chronicle, Iraq, 1st millennium BCE

when they excavated Hattusa in central Anatolia (modern Turkey). In Hattusa, an ancient city with grand stone palaces and temples built high on a rocky plateau, they found more than 25,000 cuneiform tablets that tell about a people called the Hittites, who lived in the land of Hatti. So the "Man of Hatti" who marched against Akkad and brought an end to the Babylonian dynasty must have been a Hittite.

In 1595, Hatti wasn't yet a great power, though it became one later. It controlled only a small part of what is now central Turkey. Yet somehow this small kingdom, led by King Mursili, conquered the capital of the ancient Mesopotamian empire, Babylon. A later Hittite leader described Mursili's victories: "He went to [the city of] Aleppo and . . . destroyed Aleppo and brought captives . . . to Hattusa. . . . Later he marched to Babylon and destroyed Babylon, and . . . brought captives and possessions of Babylon to Hattusa."

After Mursili's troops destroyed Aleppo, in northern Syria, they followed the path of the Euphrates River and marched all the way down to Babylon. Did the Hittites have to fight their way to Babylon or did the native peoples just let them pass through their land? And *why* did the Hittites want to conquer Babylon in the first place? They didn't have an empire yet. In fact, after their surprise attack, they turned around and went home again. They didn't even leave a Hittite leader in charge of Babylon when they left. Did they raid the city for its wealth? Or did Mursili just want to prove what a great warrior-king he was?

These are murky questions. It's clear, though, that the Babylonians suffered a terrible fate. Their Hittite enemies took their city god Marduk and his goddess wife from the temple. (Gods, like humans, were believed to have wives. These goddesses sometimes had their own temples right next to those of their husbands.) This would have terrified the Babylonians who believed that the spirit of the gods lived in

" Telipinu, Telipinu Proclamation, 16th century BCE

At the end of the third millennium BCE, expert metalworkers from Anatolia created this bronze rein ring for a wagon or chariot pulled by donkeys or horses.

the statues themselves. With their "statue-bodies" gone, the gods could no longer protect the city and its people.

Although no one wrote about the disaster at the time, we can imagine the fear, sadness, and confusion that the Babylonians suffered. They had lived in comfort, with security and power. Then, without warning, people who spoke a strange language and wore strange clothing stormed their city, looted their gold and silver, and destroyed their buildings. Many people must have died fighting to protect their homes and families. Men, women, and children were taken captive. With ropes tied around their wrists, they were driven from their homes and forced to abandon their possessions. After marching for weeks to the foreign land of their captors, they became slaves.

The very gods whom the Babylonians depended upon to watch over them now belonged to their enemies (though they were eventually returned to their home city). For the Babylonians who had been taken hostage as well as for those who had been left behind in the ruined city, it was the end of the world they had known.

Mursili and the kings who followed him on the Hittite throne saw military conquests as a basic part of their royal job and carefully recorded their accomplishments on clay tablets. These year-by-year accounts almost look like history writing except they are one-sided. They mention only the kings' accomplishments, ignoring their mistakes or military defeats. Mursili's father, Hattusili, for example, boasted, "No one had crossed the river Euphrates, but I the Great King . . . crossed it on foot, and my army crossed it after me on foot. Sargon also crossed it [long ago]."

> Hattusili, Annals of Hattusili, 17th century BCE

Like his father who compared himself to the ancient king, when Mursili conquered Babylon, he must have thought that he was on the way to becoming the next **Sargon**—a warrior-king whose name would never be forgotten. But Mursili's luck didn't last. Soon after he returned from Mesopotamia, his sister's husband murdered him and declared himself king. The plot had probably been hatched during the king's long absence. Later, Mursili's assassin was murdered by another wanna-be king. Assassinations of

> King Sargon ruled Mesopotamia 700 years before Mursili's reign in Hatti, but his adventures were so entertaining that they even appeared in Hittite legends.

Hittite kings became common after this and weakened the country for almost two hundred years.

The century from 1595 to around 1500 BCE was a troubled time throughout the Near East. The Hittites had left no one in charge in Babylon, so Mesopotamia drifted, leaderless, until a mysterious group called the Kassites took control. (They came from a land they didn't identify and spoke a language they never wrote down.) After their victory, the days of Mesopotamia's greatness appeared to be over. But by 1400 BCE, the picture had changed again. The Kassites had completely merged into Mesopotamian society, adopting the local dress, gods, language, and customs. Mesopotamia had regained its strength under its Kassite kings. Mean-

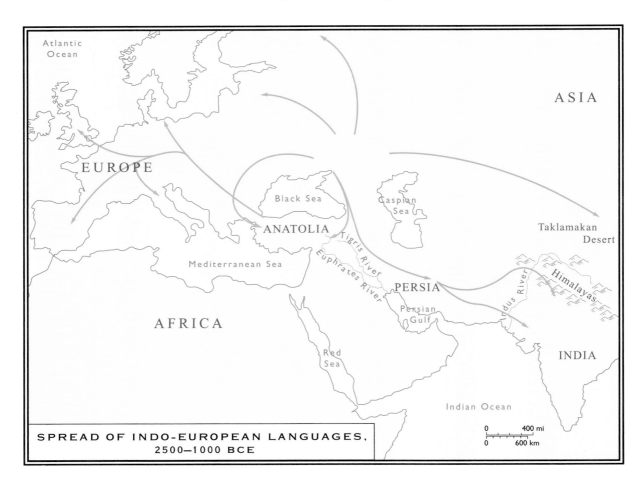

SPREAD OF INDO-EUROPEAN LANGUAGES,
2500–1000 BCE

while, the Hittites had gained control over a large empire. Their powerful kings were considered to be the equals of the rulers of Egypt and Mesopotamia.

What's really interesting about the Hittites is the fact that their language teaches us a lot about the origin of many modern languages, including English. Hittite is distantly related to English—like a 13th cousin, 10 times removed. It belongs in the family of languages that includes Greek, Latin, English, Spanish, German, French, Italian, Farsi (the language spoken in modern Iran), and several modern South Asian languages, to name a few. Of these languages, known as Indo-European languages, Hittite was the first to be written down. It was written on clay tablets in the cuneiform script that began in Mesopotamia.

Scholars have shown that the Indo-Europeans' ancestors—those who spoke Indo-European languages—all spoke the same language at first, because certain words in the various Indo-European languages are almost the same. For example, our English word *daughter* was *duatra* in Hittite, almost the same word. And many other modern languages have similar words that mean "daughter," such as *tochter* in German, *dukte* in Lithuanian, and *dokhtar* in Farsi.

Where the Indo-Europeans actually came from originally

A FAMILY OF LANGUAGES

A family of languages is much like a family of people who come from the same ancestor. This means that thousands of years ago, the people who spoke the ancestor language, known to us as proto-Indo-European, were related to each other—a huge family with thousands of cousins. Before these peoples began to write their words, the family groups began to spread out. Some traveled far from their homeland, immigrating across Europe, the Near East, South Asia, and as far as western China.

Greek, Latin, Hittite, Sanskrit, and Tocharian all developed from this same ancestor.

INDO-EUROPEAN COUSINS	
deity	Hittite *diu*, French *dieu*, Greek *dios*, Latin *dues*, Spanish *dio*
eat	Hittite *ed*, German *essen*, Greek *edo* (I eat), Latin *edere*
is	Hittite *es*, French *est*, German *ist*, Latin *est*, Spanish *esta*
new	Hittite *newa*, French *nouveau*, Latin *novos*, Sanskrit *navas*, Spanish *nuevo*
water	Hittite *watar*, German *wasser*, Russian *woda*
we	Hittite *wes*, Czech *ve*, German *wir*

Many Indo-European languages, such as Hittite and English, include words that are similar to each other—words that are descended from ancient Indo-European words.

THE OLD BABYLONIAN EMPIRE

1900 BCE
Amorite dynasty founded; Old Babylonian period begins

1792–1750 BCE
Hammurabi creates Old Babylonian Empire

1775–1761 BCE
Zimri-Lim of Mari, Syria reigns

1749–1712 BCE
Samsu-iluna of Babylon reigns

1650 BCE
Foreign invaders destroy Sippar

1625–1595 BCE
Samsu-ditana of Babylon reigns

1595 BCE
Mursili of Hatti attacks Babylon; Old Babylonian Empire ends

This bearded young man wears a peaceful smile. We don't know who he was—only that he was a prominent Kassite. Only gods and important mortals were depicted in Mesopotamian works of art.

is not known for certain. Historians, archaeologists, and language experts have argued about it for decades. Many of them now think that the original homeland of the Indo-Europeans was near the Caspian Sea in what is now Russia. The people in this region knew how to use the wheel. Perhaps they had learned this skill from the Mesopotamians. They also had tamed wild horses for use on their farms and in battle. These skills gave them an advantage over less advanced peoples whom they met as they migrated to new places.

As the Indo-Europeans spread out, beginning around 2500 BCE, they took their horses and wagons with them. They settled in new areas, farmed, and intermarried with the local people. Gradually, their languages changed—influenced by the local languages where the people now lived. No longer was there a single Indo-European language.

The descendants of those original Indo-European speakers now speak dozens of different languages. All languages, including English, change constantly, Some words disappear—whatever happened to "corset" and "persnickety?" Some words change—-in the 17th century, "painful" meant "careful." And look what happened to "cool." Still other words appear in the language, brand-new, such as "television," "surfboard," and "antibiotic."

CHAPTER 17

BRIDES AND BROTHER KINGS

DIPLOMACY AND THE GREAT POWERS

Excited people must have jammed the streets of Thebes—standing on tiptoe, straining to see the young princess who would soon become a queen. Attendants carried her in a tall, covered chair. It was 1350 BCE, and Tadu-Heba was on her way to the palace to marry Egypt's aging king. She had traveled from Syria all the way to Egypt's capital city with servants and thousands of beautiful gifts, including chariots, ceremonial weapons made of gold, four beautiful horses, thousands of bows and arrows, and four suits of armor. Her father, Tushratta, wrote to Egypt's king, Nimmureya, who was also known as Amenhotep III: "It is all of these wedding-gifts, . . . that Tushratta, the king of Mittani, gave to Nimmureya, the king of Egypt. . . . He gave them at the same time that he gave Tadu-Heba, his daughter, to Egypt and to Nimmureya to be his wife."

Although Tushratta described the wedding gifts as being for Egypt's king, in fact, most of them were for the bride—a rich dowry from her doting father. He sent her off with woolen shirts, leather shoes, gloves, sashes, a silver washbasin, combs, spoons, trays, warm blankets and bedspreads, scented oils, five sculpted dogs made of silver, and hundreds of other things that she might need or want in her new life. She also brought elegant jewelry with her, such as an iron bracelet covered with six shekels worth of gold and bright-blue stones (lapis lazuli) set in a bird pattern. The princess was marrying the most powerful man in the whole region, and she would need to dress the part.

The people of Egypt celebrated the marriage between Tadu-Heba and Nimmureya. For them, the union promised peace between Egypt and the distant land of Mittani, a kingdom in northern Mesopotamia and Syria. But for Tadu-

❝ Tushratta, letter to wife of Amenhotep III, 14th century BCE

In this cuneiform letter, Mittani's King Tushratta begs Queen Tiy for a gold statue of his daughter, a young wife of the Egyptian king.

IRON—NOT JUST FOR HAMMERS AND NAILS

Near Eastern peoples were the first to use iron. Scholars used to think that the Hittites used iron weapons, and that this gave them an advantage over their enemies. The Hittites did mine iron ore in Anatolia, but this early iron was good only for decorative things, such as jewelry. Around 1200 BCE, when the Hittites were no longer a major power, other peoples figured out how to separate iron ore from its impurities so that it would be strong enough to be used for weapons and tools. This discovery marks the beginning of the Iron Age and the end of the Bronze Age.

Heba, it was the end of all that she had known. She had traveled for many miles over land and by boat. What must she have felt as she entered Egypt and saw its wonders—the massive Sphinx and the huge triangular pyramids? And how did she feel as the moment drew near when she would meet her husband for the first time? Was she eager to become queen of this rich, important land, or was she afraid, so far from her family? She must have known that Amenhotep spoke no Hurrian, her own language. And she certainly knew that he already had many wives. Her own aunt was one of them.

Marriages between royalty of different countries, such as the one between Princess Tadu-Heba and King Amenhotep III, were common at this time. Amenhotep's wives also included Babylonian princesses and a princess from Anatolia. The king had so many wives that he could

Paintings, including this one of a bird landing in a marsh, decorated the walls of Amenhotep's palace, where Tadu-Heba came to live.

The Egyptian god Bes clenches his fists. Although he looks fierce, Tadu-Heba might have prayed to him when she was married to the Egyptian king, because Bes was the Egyptian god of marriage.

not always keep track of them. One Babylonian king wrote to Amenhotep asking what had happened to his sister: "Here you are asking for my daughter in marriage, but my sister…is [already] with you, and no one… seems…to know if now she is alive or…dead."

Perhaps to make sure that Tadu-Heba didn't get lost in Amenhotep's collection of wives, her father sent her regular gifts and even asked the Egyptian king to send him a gold statue of her, though, as far as we know, he never received it.

In King Tushratta's day, the kings of Egypt, Mittani, Babylon, and Hatti were at peace with one another. After centuries of fighting for control of land, they had formed a close-knit group known as the Great Kings. The fifth great power, the island of Alashiya (now known as Cyprus) managed to get in the Great King club because it had something that all the others wanted: copper. Copper, a major ingredient in bronze, was needed everywhere to make weapons and tools.

Egypt was the richest of the five great powers because it had gold. But the others had goods to exchange, too: tin, textiles, horses, silver, iron, glass, perfumes, wooden objects, and lapis lazuli—a dark blue stone used in jewelry. The five kings called one another "brother" as a way of claiming friendship and ensuring peace between their kingdoms. They kept their messengers busy carrying letters and gifts back and forth between them. Their wives wrote to one another, too.

Long before Tushratta, around 1500 BCE, a new dynasty had come to power in Northern Mesopotamia and Syria. These kings were Tadu-Heba's ancestors, and they created the kingdom of Mittani. Their people spoke many different languages, but the kings of Mittani used Akkadian as

> Burra-buriyash, letter to Amenhotep III, 14th century BCE

SIMILAR, BUT NOT THE SAME

Egypt's religious beliefs were different from the rest of the Near Eastern world's. Whereas most Near Easterners saw their kings as powerful human beings, the Egyptians worshiped their kings—called pharaohs—as gods. And Egypt's writing system was completely different, too: they used hieroglyphs rather than cuneiform signs. Like cuneiform, hieroglyphs stood for sounds, whole words, or symbols. But there are differences. In hieroglyphs, vowels were not expressed in syllables, as they were in cuneiform. Also, formal hieroglyphs look more like pictures than cuneiform's wedge-shaped signs.

WHY DON'T YOU WRITE ME?

The five Great Kings never met face to face, and some weren't even sure where the other kings' countries were. For example, when a Babylonian king became ill, he sent a note to the Egyptian king to complain that the Egyptian king had not sent him a "Get Well" note. (This letter was found at Amarna, in Egypt.) An Egyptian messenger explained that Egypt was too far away for the king to have known his brother king was ill. The Babylonian king found this hard to believe. It was, in fact, a journey of more than 1,500 miles from Babylon to Amarna. If a messenger had traveled 20 miles a day, taking the fastest possible route between the two countries, it would have taken him two and a half months to get to the foreign court, and another two and a half months to bring a message back.

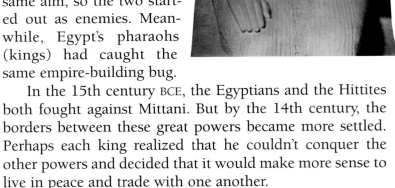

If the Egyptian king had a statue made of Tadu-Heba, it would have been in this style, with the princess fashionably dressed in an elaborate wig and a pleated dress.

their official language. In fact, Akkadian became the official language of diplomacy—the language used by palace scribes and ambassadors whenever they talked with officials from other lands.

The kings of Mittani wanted more land and especially wanted to control a port on the Mediterranean Sea. The Hittites had the same aim, so the two started out as enemies. Meanwhile, Egypt's pharaohs (kings) had caught the same empire-building bug.

In the 15th century BCE, the Egyptians and the Hittites both fought against Mittani. But by the 14th century, the borders between these great powers became more settled. Perhaps each king realized that he couldn't conquer the other powers and decided that it would make more sense to live in peace and trade with one another.

The five "brother" kings enjoyed a long era of friendship. The 14th century BCE is sometimes known as the International Age of ancient Near Eastern history. We know so much about it because all the kings wrote to one another in Akkadian using cuneiform script on baked clay tablets, which are almost indestructible, especially in the dry climate of the Egyptian desert. Tadu-Heba married Amenhotep during this time of peace.

The International Age came to a sudden end 150 years later. The reason isn't clear. But documents found at the ancient city of Ugarit give us a glimpse of the disaster, just before it happened.

Ugarit, one of the great trading centers of the Hittite empire, nestled in a valley in Syria with a view of the blue Mediterranean. One day, in 1185 BCE, Ugarit's king, Ammurapi, saw an unfamiliar warship in the harbor. Then another one sailed into view. As more ships appeared on the horizon, Ammurapi grew increasingly frightened. Who were these strangers who threatened the city? The king was helpless. He had no troops to send against the enemy. He had already sent his land forces to help another Hittite king, and his navy was away too.

Ammurapi dashed off a desperate message to the king of Carchemish, an ancient city on the Euphrates in Syria.

Green fields surround the ancient city of Ugarit, with the blue Mediterranean not far away. Ugarit was a thriving center for trade, and at its center were great temples to the gods Baal and Dagan.

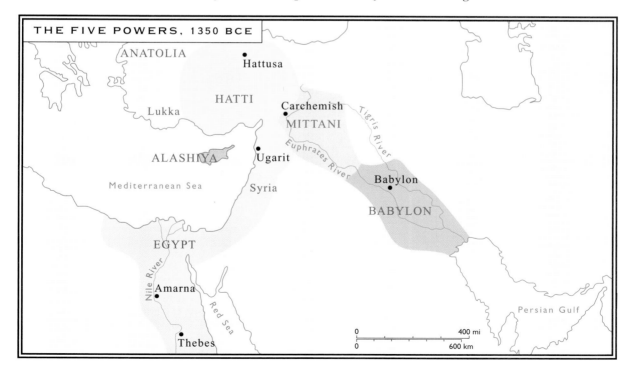

THE FIVE POWERS, 1350 BCE

ANATOLIA

Hattusa

Lukka

HATTI

Carchemish

MITTANI

Tigris River

ALASHIYA

Ugarit

Euphrates River

Babylon

Mediterranean Sea

Syria

BABYLON

EGYPT

Nile River

Amarna

Red Sea

Persian Gulf

0   400 mi

0   600 km

Thebes

Ammurapi explained to his fellow king the looming danger and begged for help. As Ammurapi waited for his messenger to come back, more ships arrived until seven enemy ships lurked in the harbor.

Ammurapi's spirits must have sunk when he read the king's response:

> As for what you have written to me: "Ships of the enemy have been seen at sea," well, you must remain firm. Indeed for your part, where are your troops...? Are they not stationed near you?...Surround your towns with ramparts. Have your troops and chariots enter there, and await the enemy with great determination.

Ammurapi needed troops, not advice. He had no way to bring his men and chariots home in time. The people of Ugarit—merchants and farmers, craftsmen, and priests—must have been worried, too. Their town had enjoyed years of wealth and ease. But now they could see mysterious enemy ships waiting to attack, like hawks eyeing their prey.

The ships landed, and the invaders swarmed in, setting fire to houses and buildings. They looted and stole from the citizens not only of Ugarit itself, but of the surrounding cities as well. The citizens may have grabbed a few valuables, but basically they just ran, abandoning their homes. The enemies eventually left, but Ugarit was in ruins.

A skilled Syrian craftsman created this gold bowl, with its three circular scenes showing lions, bulls, ibexes, and fantastic animals. Archaeologists found it in Ugarit.

About this same time, another messenger arrived by sea. Did he bring good news? Were Ammurapi's troops returning perhaps, or was a neighboring king promising to send help? If these were the king's hopes, they were dashed on the rocks of disappointment. The message was from the king of the island of Alashiya, begging for help. He, too, was under attack. Ammurapi wrote back, calling him "father" as a term of respect because he was one of the five Great Kings:

> My father,...the enemy's ships came here; my cities were burned...Does not my father know that all my troops and chariots are in the Land of Hatti, and all my ships are in the Land of Lukka?...Thus, the

country is abandoned to itself.... The seven ships of the enemy that came here inflicted great damage upon us.

Archaeologists discovered this letter and the one from the king of Carchemish in the 1950s as they excavated the remains of Ugarit. The archaeological evidence showed that the city had, in fact, burned around 1185 BCE and was never rebuilt.

Ugarit was not the only city that was mysteriously destroyed in the early years of the 12th century BCE. The Hittites' magnificent capital, the city of Hattusa, was also burned and abandoned around the same time. The invaders may have been refugees from another part of the Mediterranean, perhaps related to a group of people who attacked Egypt around the same time. The Egyptians called them the Sea Peoples.

The Near East was a changed place by 1100 BCE. The kingdoms of Mittani, Hatti, and Alashiya were gone. Egypt was struggling to stay in one piece, and Babylonia was in decline. Trade had shriveled to nearly nothing. For several hundred years, there were no great powers in the Near East. The glory days were over. Survival became the name of the game.

THE INTERNATIONAL AGE

1595–1500 BCE
Near East in turmoil

1500 BCE
Kassites in power in Babylonia; kingdom of Mittani begins; Hittite Empire grows

1387–1350 BCE
Amenhotep III reigns in Egypt; height of International Age; diplomatic marriages between Great Kings of Egypt, Babylonia, Mittani, and Hatti

1185 BCE
Invaders destroy Canaanite towns; Hittite capital is destroyed; Hittite Empire collapses

1176 BCE
Sea Peoples attack Egypt; International Age ends

Massive gateposts, carved into the shape of roaring lions, still stand at Hattusa. Invaders destroyed many of its city walls around 1200 BCE.

CHAPTER 18

KING DAVID AND HIS FAMILY

THE SETTLEMENTS AND MOVEMENTS OF THE ISRAELITES

❝ A PHOENICIAN
KING'S INSCRIPTION,
THE MOABITE
STONE, AND THE
BOOKS OF RUTH,
FIRST SAMUEL,
FIRST KINGS AND
PROVERBS

❝ Azitawadda, royal inscription, possibly 10th or 9th century BCE

The Phoenician kingdom that Azitawadda ruled was small, but his ego was huge. He proclaimed his own greatness in a royal inscription: "I am Azitawadda, blessed of (the god) Baal...I have made peace with every king. Yes, every king considers me his father because of my goodness and my wisdom and the kindness of my heart."

Later in the inscription, Azitawadda bragged that, thanks to him, his people always had plenty to eat, that he had built a new city, and pleased the gods with his sacrifices. He believed that "the name of Azitawadda shall endure forever like the name of the sun and the moon."

But Azitawadda *was* forgotten for thousands of years until archaeologists discovered his inscription in the 1940s. We don't know exactly when he ruled. And we know even less about most of the other Near Eastern kings who ruled during his time. We don't even know the names of most of them. With the collapse of the five great powers, the Levant—modern Israel, Jordan, Lebanon, and the Palestinian territories—became home to many smaller kingdoms.

The years between 1100 and 900 BCE are called a "dark age" because so few texts survive to shed light on what was going on. In fact, historians would have very little to say about these two centuries in the Levant if it weren't for the writings of the people of Israel.

Israel and its neighboring kingdoms were alike in many ways. They all traded goods with one another, but sometimes fought over land. Their kings led troops, rebuilt cities, levied taxes, and tried to keep order at home. Sheepherders, who moved from place to place with their flocks, had founded several of these kingdoms, including Israel. One of these groups, the Arameans, became a major power in the Levant and controlled a large stretch of land. Their language, Aramaic, spread during the dark age and afterward. Aramaic became the language spoken by most of the Near Eastern peoples and was still spoken in the region more than a thousand years later. The people of Israel spoke Hebrew, which was similar to their neighbors' languages.

Despite many similarities, the Israelites differed from the other peoples of the Levant in this important way: they thought it was important to *write down* their history. They didn't just list their kings or copy a few inscriptions. Just the opposite: they wrote long books about who they were, what they did, and what they believed. Many different authors penned these books over hundreds of years. Eventually, editors put these texts into one book that became known as the Hebrew Bible. Its words have been copied, studied, and discussed, from the time it was written until now. This collection of stories, histories, hymns, and prophecies never had to be excavated or rediscovered, because it was never lost or forgotten. So although we have almost no records from the Arameans or the other communities in the Levant, and little archaeological evidence, we can learn a lot about the Israelites' lives and beliefs from the Hebrew Bible.

The Israelites were said to be newcomers to the Levant

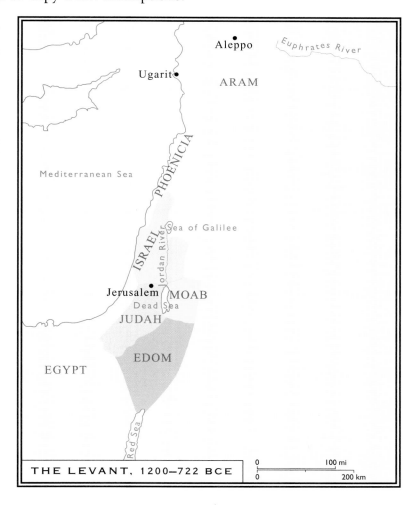

THE LEVANT, 1200–722 BCE

THE STORY OF RUTH

The Hebrew Bible's Book of Ruth tells the story of a young Canaanite woman who lived in the land of Moab with her husband, an Israelite. Ruth became a widow when she was still young. Her husband's mother, Naomi, decided to go back to Israel after her son's death.

The biblical writers tell us that Naomi kissed Ruth goodbye and set out, intending to go to her homeland alone. But Ruth insisted on going with her. "Don't ask me to leave you," she said, "for where you go, I will go, and where you live, I will live. Your people will be my people and your God my God. Where you die, I will die, and there will I be buried." So Ruth went with Naomi to Israel, where she married an Israelite landowner named Boaz. Ruth and Boaz had children, and Ruth became the great-grandmother of David, one of Israel's greatest kings.

around 1200 BCE. According to the Hebrew Bible, after a dramatic escape from slavery and a long journey from Egypt, the Israelites invaded the land of Canaan, where they hoped to settle. At the same time that the Israelites were moving into Canaan, the Philistines were invading too. (The Philistines had probably been one of the Sea Peoples, who attacked Egypt in the 12th century BCE.)

For a time, the Levant churned with these invasions. It's a small area, about half the size of California, and it was overrun with people speaking many different languages and following many different customs. The invading tribes did not fight over customs, though. They battled over land. The newly arrived Israelites and Philistines first fought the local peoples, whom we call Canaanites, and then they fought each other.

The part of the Levant that was good for farming was just a narrow strip of land squeezed between the Mediterranean Sea in the west and mountains and desert in the east. Traders passed back and forth through this land, going from Egypt to Anatolia and from Mesopotamia to the Mediterranean. So the land, although it was small, had the potential to grow rich from farming and trade.

The biblical description of the Israelites' early years begins during the dark age, when the Israelites were organized into 12 tribes. Belonging to a particular tribe gave people a sense of safety as they moved into the new land, which had been known as Canaan but which they called Israel.

At first, the tribes had no single leader, uniting under a military ruler only when they had to fight against neighboring peoples. But after being repeatedly defeated, the Israelites decided that they needed a king. They chose Saul. The writer of the First Book of Samuel describes him as "an impressive young man without equal among the [Israelites] . . . a head taller than the others." But the Israelites still suffered defeat at the hands of the Philistines.

Israel's second king, David, was just a shepherd boy. Despite his simple background, he could claim that the Israelites' god Yahweh chose him to be king because Israel's most respected religious leader, Samuel, had anointed him

Samuel anoints David. This Syrian painting was made over a thousand years after David's lifetime, and his story is still important to Jews to this day.

COUSINLY BOOKS

The Hebrew Bible was the holy book of the ancient Israelites, who were the ancestors of modern Jews. Christianity developed more than a thousand years after Israel first flourished. Christians later adopted the Hebrew Bible and called it the Old Testament. Collected Christian writings eventually became the New Testament. Together, the two Testaments form the Christian Bible. The Quran, the holy book of the Muslims, also includes many stories from the Hebrew Bible and honors many of the same leaders, such as Abraham, Isaac, and Moses.

by pouring oil on his head. The people loved David and told stories about his adventures, which have come down to us in the Hebrew Bible.

In one of these stories, a hugely tall giant—a Philistine named Goliath—wearing full bronze armor and carrying a large spear and a sword, challenged the Israelites to "Choose a man and have him come down to me. If he is able to . . . kill me, we will become your subjects, but if I . . . kill him, you will . . . serve us." David, just a boy, was the only one brave enough to take up the challenge, even though he was much smaller than the giant. David's only weapons were five smooth stones and a slingshot.

66 I Samuel, Hebrew Bible

> As the Philistine moved closer to attack him, David ran quickly toward the battle line . . . Reaching into his bag and taking out a stone, he slung it and struck the Philistine. . . . The stone sank into his forehead and he fell facedown on the ground. So David triumphed over the Philistine . . . and killed him.

A man takes aim with a sling, just as David did in the Hebrew Bible's story about David and the giant, Goliath. This Syrian sculpture was made about 200 years after David's time.

According to the biblical story, David moved up in the Israelites' army, became king, and united the land under his control. He ruled over Canaanites, Hittites (those who were now living in the Levant), and Philistines as well as his own Israelite people. He conquered a Canaanite city called Jerusalem, made it his capital, and built his royal palace there.

David brought the Israelites' most sacred object into Jerusalem: an elaborate box called the Ark of the Covenant. The ark was made from a fine, beautiful wood, overlaid with gold. Inside were treasures of the Israelite people, including two stone tablets upon which were written the Ten Commandments—the most holy laws of the Israelite people.

After David's death, his son Solomon took over the kingdom. The biblical record describes Solomon as a wise king whose reign was both peaceful and prosperous. He built a new palace for himself and an elaborate temple to Yahweh, where the Ark of the Covenant was kept. Solomon traded with other countries, became very rich, and married many foreign princesses. (The biblical story says that he had seven hundred wives!)

Solomon traded with the Phoenicians, Azitawadda's people, who lived on the Mediterranean coast just north of

"Do not work to gain riches.... As soon as your eyes light upon [wealth], it is gone, for suddenly it takes ... wings, flying like an eagle."

—Book of Proverbs, Hebrew Bible

"Riches ... have made themselves wings like geese and are flown away to the heavens."

—Anonymous Egyptian author, "The Instruction of Amen-em-opet," 7th or 6th century BCE

Israel. The Phoenicians were expert sailors, and their boats could carry them all the way across the Mediterranean. Eventually they established colonies as far away as southern Spain and North Africa, and they became very wealthy from the trade that they controlled. According to the Hebrew Bible, Solomon bought timber from the Phoenicians for his building projects, and he also hired skilled Phoenician sailors and laborers.

After Solomon's death, around 922 BCE, the kingdom of Israel broke in two. The southern part of the land chose Solomon's son as its king. These people kept Jerusalem as their capital city, but changed the kingdom's name to Judah, which was the name of the Israelite tribe that lived there. The northern part of the kingdom kept the name of Israel but chose a new king and a new capital city. For two hundred years, the two kingdoms shared a border. Sometimes they were friendly with one another; at other times they were at war.

In 1868, a British missionary traveling through the Near East was shown a stone with an inscription written by a Canaanite king of Moab, a kingdom near Israel. Historians were excited to learn about this stone, because the ancient inscription mentions a king of Israel named Omri, whom they had only read about in the Hebrew Bible: "the Israelites in the camp . . . proclaimed Omri, the commander of the army, king over Israel that very day there in the camp." According to the inscription, Omri had defeated the Moabites, a victory that the Moabite king blamed on the anger of his own god, Chemosh. "As for Omri, king of Israel, he humbled Moab many years, for [the god] Chemosh was angry at his land."

King Omri doesn't play a big role in the Hebrew Bible, but the Assyrians, who later controlled a powerful empire in the Near East, saw him as the founder of a dynasty of Israelite kings. In fact, the Assyrians called Israel "the House of Omri." With the discovery of this inscription, written during Omri's own time, historians at last had hard evidence that an early king of Israel actually lived and reigned, just as the biblical records claim.

THE WISDOM OF AN ANCIENT KING

For centuries, King Solomon has gotten credit for many of the wise sayings in the Hebrew Bible's Book of Proverbs. In fact, no one knows whether he actually wrote them or not. They may even have been written after his death, but the advice in Proverbs 15:1 is good, regardless of who wrote it: "A soft answer turns away wrath, but a harsh word stirs up anger."

❝ I Kings, Hebrew Bible

❝ Mesha, Moabite Stone, around 830 BCE

CHAPTER 19

THE BOOK OF GENESIS AND A MESOPOTAMIAN POEM

ONE GOD, MANY STORIES
THE BELIEFS OF THE ISRAELITES

Children often ask, "Where did I come from?" Groups of people, too—ancient tribes and modern families—have asked similar questions: "Where did we come from?" and "How did life begin?" The answers have given birth to thousands of legends, folk songs, and histories. The creation stories of the ancient Israelites were passed down for hundreds of years, then finally written down. The first book of the Hebrew Bible, Genesis, opens with a poem about the creation of the world.

Genesis, Hebrew Bible

> In the beginning, God created the heavens and the earth. The earth was without form...and darkness was upon the face of the deep....And God said, "Let there be light," and there was light....And God saw that the light was good; and God separated the light from the darkness. God called the light Day, and the darkness he called Night.

The Israelites believed in a god named Yahweh who cared about the earth and its people. In the story that begins in the second chapter of **Genesis**, Yahweh created the first man, Adam, and the first woman, Eve, and gave them everything in the world for their own use. All he asked was that they obey him. In this story, Yahweh put Adam and Eve in the beautiful Garden of Eden, a paradise of trees and rivers, and told them that they could eat the fruit of any tree except for one. Adam and Eve obeyed until a snake tempted Eve to taste the forbidden fruit. She fell for his slithery words and convinced Adam to take a bite, too. Because they disobeyed Yahweh, Adam and Eve had to leave the Garden of Eden and were no longer given everything they wanted. Now they had to work.

A later Israelite story describes a time when Yahweh

Genesis and *genealogy* come from related Latin and Greek words. Genesis means beginning or birth and comes from *genus*, the Latin word for origin or race. Genealogy, from the Greek *genealogia*, traces a family's ancestors.

Archaeologists uncover a clay coffin at an excavation site in Israel. The coffin is shaped like a human, an idea that came from Egypt.

said, "I have decided to make an end of all flesh, for the earth is filled with violence." In his anger at mankind, Yahweh decided to destroy all creation in a terrible flood, saving only a good man named Noah and his family. According to Genesis, Yahweh told Noah to build "an ark of . . . wood; make rooms in the ark, and cover it inside and out with tar." Noah loaded the ark with a male and female of every creature on Earth. Once he, his family, and all the animals were inside, the rain began. "The flood continued for 40 days upon the earth . . . and bore up the ark, and it rose high above the earth."

66 Genesis, Hebrew Bible

The floodwater destroyed everything and dry land did not reappear for 150 days. When it was finally safe to leave the ark, life on Earth began again. The Israelites believed that the rainbow was the symbol of Yahweh's promise that he would never again destroy the whole Earth by flood.

The Mesopotamians had a similar flood story that was written down long before the Hebrew flood story was recorded. In this story, too, the household of one man, Ut-napishtim, was saved. Like Noah, Ut-napishtim was warned about the flood, and was told to build a boat and fill it with animals. Once the boat was ready, "the weather changed,

66 "Myth of Atrahasis," Iraq, 17th century BCE

The Phoenician scribes, who lived to the north of Israel, found a way to write their language using fewer signs than the hundreds that were needed in Mesopotamian cuneiform. Instead of having a sign for each syllable, they chose a sign for each consonant. But this early alphabet was not the first. Scholars have found inscriptions in the Sinai Peninsula, near Egypt, from around 1600 BCE that were written in what they believe was an even earlier alphabet, invented by other Canaanites—the great-great-grandparent of the alphabet we use today.

The Israelites used an alphabet that was adopted from the Phoenician one. It wasn't until much later that the Greeks, who also borrowed the Phoenician alphabet, added letters to represent vowels.

66 Genesis, Hebrew Bible

and [the storm god] Adad began to roar in the clouds . . . the winds were furious as he set forth."

One big difference between the two stories comes in the reason for the flood. In the Hebrew story, Yahweh punished the people because they did things that were wrong. In the Mesopotamian story, the god Enlil became angry because, "The clamor of mankind has become burdensome to me, I am losing sleep to their uproar." Humans made so much noise, they kept him awake! The storm began at his command.

The two peoples' ideas about their gods, Yahweh and Enlil, were very different from one another. And the religions that developed around these gods were different, too. The Israelites who wrote the Bible believed in one god who expected them to worship him by living good lives. The Mesopotamians believed in lots of gods who expected people to serve and care for them. Their chief god Enlil often grew impatient with human beings, but Ea, the kind god of fresh water, sometimes went behind Enlil's back to protect people from Enlil's fury. (It was Ea who warned Ut-napishtim about the flood.) The god of the Israelites combined the traits of Enlil and Ea. Like Enlil, he sent the great flood, but, like Ea, he found a way to protect and preserve life on Earth.

These two flood stories are too much alike not to be related to one another. A very ancient tradition probably lies behind both of them, but each culture shaped the story to fit its own beliefs. People told and retold both stories before finally writing them down.

According to the authors of Genesis, Noah's family began a whole new era on Earth after the floodwaters went down and the family was able to leave the ark. The Israelites believed that, at first, all humans spoke the same language. When they began to build a huge tower of baked bricks, Yahweh grew worried that the people might become proud and rebellious. He said "If, as one people speaking the same language, they have begun to do this, then nothing . . . will be impossible for them." So he caused them to speak in different languages. Now the people babbled at one another and could no longer understand each other or work together. They never finished their tower, which became known as

the Tower of Babel, and soon scattered to different lands.

In the pages of Genesis, after the stories of creation, Adam and Eve, the flood, and the Tower of Babel, we meet an old man named Abraham, whom the Israelites honored as their original ancestor. The Israelites believed that long, long ago Yahweh gave Abraham instructions and a promise: "Go from your country... to the land that I will show you. And I will make of you a great nation, and I will bless you, and make your name great." According to tradition, Abraham's two sons, Isaac and Ishmael, became the "fathers" of two peoples: the Israelites and the Arabs.

Through these stories, the biblical writers explained how different families and different tribes living near one anoth-

A 16th-century CE artist created this imaginary impression of the Tower of Babel, with its top in the clouds. A minaret built centuries earlier in Iraq might have inspired him.

📖 Genesis, Hebrew Bible

The story of Joseph and his brothers was set to music in a modern musical, Joseph and the Amazing Technicolor Dreamcoat. *The Hebrew Bible says that Jacob gave his son Joseph a "coat of many colors" because he was Jacob's favorite— and this made the brothers jealous.*

er sometimes got along but sometimes fought, just as siblings in some families do.

Isaac's grandson Joseph (Abraham's great-grandson) stars in a story from the Book of Genesis that count- less people have enjoyed. When Joseph was a teenager, his brothers sold him to a band of traveling merchants. The brothers hated Joseph because their father Jacob loved him best. The merchants sold Joseph to a rich Egyptian. But "the Lord was with Joseph, and he became a successful man . . . in the house of his master, the Egyptian. . . . and [his master] put him in charge over all that he had." So Joseph was in Egypt—and in power—when his brothers, desperate from famine, came to beg for grain.

Joseph's brothers didn't recognize him, but he knew who they were. At first, he hid his identity, but then "Joseph could no longer control himself . . . and he wept so loudly that the Egyptians heard him, . . . Joseph said to his brothers 'I am Joseph! Is my father still living?'" He forgave his brothers for their cruelty to him, and they all moved to Egypt to join him. According to the story, the Israelite com- munity grew and flourished. And when Joseph died at the grand old age of 110, he was buried in Egypt, never guess- ing that his people would soon be unwelcome there.

66 Genesis, Hebrew Bible

CHAPTER 20

THE LOST LAWS OF THE ISRAELITES

THE EXODUS AND THE TEN COMMANDMENTS

King Josiah came to Israel's throne when he was only eight years old. According to the biblical story in the Second Book of Kings, Josiah grew up to be a just and good king. In the 18th year of his reign, he decided to repair the old temple that King Solomon had built in Jerusalem 300 years earlier. He hired carpenters, builders, and stonemasons for the job. As it turned out, these workers did more than restore Yahweh's temple. In the course of their labors, they discovered a scroll, a rolled document, that had been lost or hidden there for decades, perhaps centuries. According to the Second Book of Kings, when they showed it to the high priest, he was overjoyed and said: "I have found the Book of the Law in the temple of the Lord."

❝ II Kings, Hebrew Bible

Historians believe that this scroll was part of the Book of Deuteronomy, the fifth book in the Hebrew Bible. Deuteronomy lists many, many laws that the Israelites believed Yahweh had given to their early leader Moses. When Josiah's secretary read the book aloud, the king was terrified and tore his clothes to show how upset he was. He knew that the Israelites had forgotten Yahweh's laws. Fearing Yahweh's

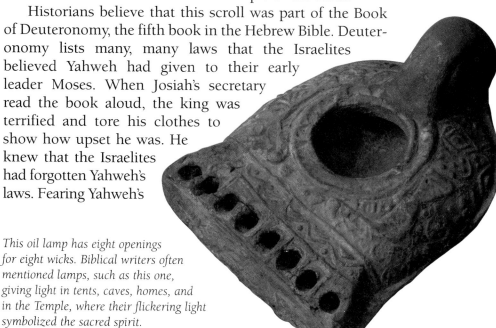

This oil lamp has eight openings for eight wicks. Biblical writers often mentioned lamps, such as this one, giving light in tents, caves, homes, and in the Temple, where their flickering light symbolized the sacred spirit.

" II Kings, Hebrew Bible

Exodus comes from the
Greek word *exodos*,
which means "departure."
The word is related to
the English word *exit*.

" Exodus, Hebrew Bible

fury, he declared, "Great is the Lord's anger that burns against us, because our fathers have not obeyed the words of this book."

According to the Book of Kings, Josiah decided that he had better give a public speech. "He went up to the temple of the Lord with the men of Judah, the people of Jerusalem,... all the people from the least to the greatest. He read...the words of the book, which had been found in the temple." The king promised to keep Yahweh's laws, and all the people who listened that day agreed to follow Yahweh.

The hero of Deuteronomy is an Israelite named Moses, but his story actually begins in **Exodus**, the second book of the Hebrew Bible. As Exodus begins, Abraham's great-grandson Joseph has died, and the Israelites have lost favor with the Egyptian pharaoh. In fact, by the time of Moses' birth, Pharaoh had enslaved the Israelites. Despite the hard work they were forced to do, the Israelite tribe grew so large that Pharaoh got nervous. He commanded the midwives, who helped women during childbirth, to kill all of the infant sons born to Israelite women. According to the biblical story, Pharaoh said: "If it is a son, you shall kill him, but if it is a daughter, she shall live."

The writer of Exodus tells how one Israelite woman managed to hide her newborn son for three months. Then, desperate, she "took a basket made of bulrushes...and put the child in it." She set it afloat on the Nile River. When Pharaoh's daughter "came down to bathe,...she saw the basket among the reeds and sent her maid to fetch it." The princess adopted the child and named him Moses.

The Israelites believed that Yahweh had chosen Moses to lead them out of their slavery in Egypt. The Book of Exodus describes how Moses, when he grew to manhood, stood up to the Egyptian ruler and demanded, "Thus says the Lord, the God of Israel, 'Let my people go.'" When Pharaoh refused to release the Israelites, Yahweh rained down punishments on the Egyptians. The Nile River turned to blood. A swarm of gnats and flies infested the earth, and the people broke out with sores all over their bodies. Finally a swarm of locusts, large grasshopper-like insects, "covered...the whole land, so that the land was darkened, and they ate all the plants... until not a green thing remained." Desperate at last, Pharaoh begged Moses to take all the people, the cattle—everything—and leave. "Get away from me," he pleaded, "never see my face again."

Unfortunately, Egyptian records from the time don't mention the Exodus of the Israelite slaves. And archaeology hasn't uncovered any evidence of their years in Egypt, nor of their dramatic departure. We have only the biblical account for evidence. But belief in the Exodus was an essential ingredient in the Israelites' idea of themselves as

In this early Christian mosaic, Moses has parted the waters of the Red Sea. The Israelites cross on dry land, but Pharaoh's soldiers, chariots, and horses drown in its churning waves.

THE JEWISH JOURNEY

around 1200 BCE
Israelites arrive in Levant

around 1020 BCE
Saul's reign begins

around 1000 BCE
David's reign begins

around 960 BCE
Solomon's reign begins

922 BCE
Israel divides into two kingdoms

722 BCE
Assyrian conquest of Israel

598–597 BCE
Jehoiakin of Judah reigns

587 BCE
Final Babylonian conquest of Judah; Babylonian exile begins

539 BCE
Jews allowed to return to Jerusalem

Moses—played by Charlton Heston in the 1956 movie The Ten Commandments—*holds the two stone tablets on which the laws were written.*

a separate and united people. Josiah's discovery of the Book of Law helped them to develop this understanding.

According to the story that Josiah read to his people, Moses led the former slaves on their journey from Egypt into Canaan. Along the way, Moses received a message from Yahweh as he stood at the top of a mountain in the wilderness. Yahweh promised that if the Israelite people would obey his commandments, he would protect them and take care of them. Moses announced to the people these ten laws, expressed as Yahweh's will:

Deuteronomy, Hebrew Bible

1. You shall have no other gods before me.
2. You shall not make . . . any graven images [idols]. . . . You shall not bow down and worship them . . .
3. You shall not take the name of the Lord your God in vain. . .
4. Observe the Sabbath day to keep it holy. . . . Six days, shall you labor and do all your work, but the seventh day is a Sabbath unto your God . . .
5. Honor your father and your mother . . .
6. You shall not kill.
7. You shall not commit adultery [by being unfaithful to your husband or wife].
8. You shall not steal.
9. You shall not bear false witness [tell lies].
10. You shall not covet [be jealous].

The people believed that Yahweh wrote these laws, known as the Ten Commandments, on two stone tablets. These commandments were absolute laws—no ifs, ands, or buts. Absolute laws never change. The Israelites believed that if they followed the laws, they would have long life, good health, many children, and prosperity. But if they disobeyed Yahweh's laws, he would be angry and punish them.

Josiah seems to have been most worried about the first commandment that tells the Israelites not to worship any gods other than Yahweh. Many Israelite people had begun to worship the gods of their Canaanite neighbors, so the king pulled down the altars and destroyed all the temples to other gods. Then he told the people to celebrate the Passover, which recalled the time when the Israelites escaped from slavery in Egypt. And Jews have celebrated the Passover holiday every year since then.

The discovery of the Book of Deuteronomy had a major effect on the Israelite people. It reminded them that they should worship just one god, Yahweh. It gave them laws to follow in their relationships to one another as well as to Yahweh, and it gave them an explanation for all the terrible things that had happened to them, such as murdered kings and terrible wars. The biblical writers believed that the Israelites' successes, such as victories in war, signaled Yahweh's approval and that disasters came when he was angry. The story of how Yahweh rewarded and punished his people is the thread that ties the writings of the Hebrew Bible together.

A god holds a shield in one hand and raises his sword in the other, ready to attack his enemies. The statue may represent the god Baal, whom the Canaanites worshiped.

HISTORIAN AT WORK:
AN INTERVIEW WITH WILLIAM H. C. PROPP

William H. C. Propp is a professor of ancient history and Judaic studies at the University of California, San Diego. He teaches courses on the civilizations and languages of the ancient Near East. He is an expert on the Hebrew Bible, and his book, Exodus 1–18, *was published in 1999.*

When did you become interested in studying the Hebrew Bible?

When I was in elementary school, I became interested in old things. It started with dinosaurs. After that, I moved on to the ancient Egyptians, the Greeks, and the Romans. In junior high, I studied Latin. Also, because my family is Jewish, I grew up with Jewish traditions and Hebrew. The stories in the Bible really grabbed me.

When you decide to study a biblical text, how do you begin?

First I have to figure out what the text is. We know that it won't be an ancient original manuscript. We don't have any texts that were actually written by the people who wrote the Bible. What we have are copies of copies of copies, written in Hebrew or in translations into Greek, Aramaic, and other languages. There are many versions of the same text, all slightly different. So we have to gather all of the evidence and try to figure out what the original words were.

What then?

Next, I look at what scholars before me thought and wrote. The Bible has been studied for more than two thousand years by Jewish scholars, Christian scholars,

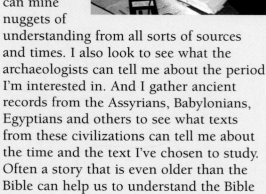

and others. I think we can mine nuggets of understanding from all sorts of sources and times. I also look to see what the archaeologists can tell me about the period I'm interested in. And I gather ancient records from the Assyrians, Babylonians, Egyptians and others to see what texts from these civilizations can tell me about the time and the text I've chosen to study. Often a story that is even older than the Bible can help us to understand the Bible and appreciate what was new about it.

You've done a lot of work on the Book of Exodus. How does the Exodus story affect the traditions of the modern Jewish community?

Every year, in the springtime, Jews retell the story of the Exodus, celebrating the time when their ancestors were finally freed from slavery in Egypt, according to tradition. We call it the Passover. We try to imagine that we are slaves, hoping for freedom. Jews are no longer slaves, so "slavery" can mean persecution, grief, or any kind of distress. But the hope is always: "This year, we are slaves. Next year, may we be free."

The Ten Commandments are absolute laws, but the Book of Deuteronomy listed other laws, too. It describes the proper ways to worship Yahweh—exactly how to perform sacrifices and how to live without angering him, including what to eat and not eat and how to behave on certain days of the week. Other laws were conditional, presenting a *particular* situation and telling how it should be handled.

Like Hammurabi's laws, many of these conditional laws say *if* a certain crime was done, *then* this should be the punishment. The conditional laws of Israel were concerned with the same types of things that Hammurabi's laws covered: agriculture, marriage, property rights, and so on. In both Mesopotamia and Israel, these practical laws were designed to allow people to solve their problems in court instead of trying to get personal revenge against those who had wronged them.

Once Josiah had rediscovered the laws, people in the Israelite community began to learn about them. And gradually, they began to pattern their lives according to Yahweh's ancient laws.

"Teach me, O Lord, the way of your commands, and I will keep them to the end. Give me understanding, that I may keep your law and follow it with my whole heart."

—Book of Psalms, Hebrew Bible

The biblical laws have had a powerful influence on history in the regions where Judaism, and later Christianity, flourished. Wise people read the laws and wrote comments about them. Others read these Commentaries, as they were called, and expanded on them. The importance of living under a set of laws became a basic principle of all Jewish and Christian societies and, later, of almost all modern countries.

We know the Israelites' stories about creation, their early leaders, and the histories of their kings because they

HOLY NAMES

To the Jews and Christians his name is Yahweh or Jehovah, but he is also referred to as God or Lord. In Hebrew, his name is Adonai; in English, God; in French, Dieu, and in German, Gott—and many other names, depending on the language of the believers.

are recorded in the Hebrew Bible. But because Yahweh is the main character in the Hebrew Bible, historians don't treat these writings as history in the usual sense. It was not until the time of the Greeks that histories were written that put humans on center stage as the "main characters."

Scholars think that the stories in the Hebrew Bible began to be written down around the time of King Solomon in the 10th century BCE. Then, for six hundred years more, people continued to collect and write stories. Scholars can tell that this happened because the authors wrote in different styles. Those who wrote later often mentioned people and events from their own times. And various authors used different vocabulary words. One, for example, always called God "Yahweh" but another called him "Elohim." Imagine a play written by Shakespeare and then a book by J. K. Rowling. Even if bits of each one were put together in the same book and the authors' names were left out, you would still know that they were written by different people. The same is true of biblical writers.

Josiah's reforms, based on his discovery of the lost scroll, were not completely successful. The Hebrew Bible records that some of the Israelites, even some of the later kings, continued to worship other gods. Eventually, though, the Israelite people came to believe that Yahweh was the only God and that he ruled over all peoples. Monotheism, belief in one God, was one of the Israelites' most important contributions to world history. Both Christians and Muslims later adopted monotheism, too. Today Jews, Christians, and Muslims all worship one God, though they call him by different names.

CHAPTER 21

ASSYRIA'S FIGHTER KINGS
WARRIORS BUILD AN EMPIRE

❝ SCULPTURES AND INSCRIPTIONS FROM A PALACE IN IRAQ, THE BLACK OBELISK OF SHALMANESER, AN ASSYRIAN KING'S INSCRIPTION, AND THE SECOND BOOK OF KINGS

A proud warrior, Ashurnasirpal II, draws his bow against an enemy town, fighting beside his men. He wears a long, woolen tunic, and his tall, "flowerpot" hat tells us that he is the Assyrian king. To his left, a soldier in a pointed helmet holds the royal shield. An attendant carries the king's quiver of arrows. Another holds a bannerlike shade to protect the commander-in-chief from the blazing desert sun. This battle scene churns with action as soldiers fight with daggers, swords, torches, and rocks. Some of the Assyrians scale the city wall on ladders while others tunnel under it. Two enemy soldiers fall to certain death, while over their heads, a vulture awaits his feast.

The Assyrians used battering rams to break through the walls of their enemies. After the battle, they would have stormed into the city, taking prisoners and stealing all the

❝ Relief from Ashurnasirpal II's palace at Calhu in Iraq, 883 BCE

Chefs prepare a feast, cooking and making wine (top), while priests sacrifice an animal in order to "read" its internal organs (bottom). The priests may be determining the best time to fight.

In ancient times, the god Ashur had the same name as the empire where he was worshiped. To avoid confusion, we call the god *Ashur*, the empire *Assyria*, and its people *Assyrians*.

wealth they could find. Soldiers were allowed to keep some of the loot, but most of it belonged to their king.

The king of the city under attack had probably refused to pay the tribute money that Assyria demanded of its subjects. Ashurnasirpal, a fierce warrior, would have destroyed the city as an example to the whole kingdom and to return the land to Assyria's control. The Assyrians believed that their victory made the god **Ashur** happy.

After the fighting and pillaging, the army would have returned, exhausted, to the camp. There, they'd be greeted by the men who traveled with the army but didn't fight: cooks, the men who groomed the horses, workers who repaired the soldiers' broken spears and armor, and divination experts who tried to interpret the will of the gods.

The army brought great wealth to the empire. When an Assyrian king conquered a city, he demanded that a "tribute" be paid each year. This payment, often made in silver, guaranteed that Assyria would protect the conquered city against its foreign enemies, but it also served as a sort of insurance policy against further attack from the Assyrians themselves. In an inscription recording the first year of his reign, Ashurnasirpal boasted that he took his enemy's silver, his gold,... dishes of copper,... the women of his palaces,... the gods together with their possessions, precious stone from the mountains, his chariot with equipment, his horses,... garments of brightly colored wool and garments of linen,... his wagons, his cattle, his sheep, his heavy spoil, which like the stars of heaven could not be counted.

Ashurnasirpal used some of the wealth from his military campaigns to build a fancy palace in his new capital city at Calhu. When the palace was finished, he threw a huge party and invited 69,574 people who feasted for 10 days. Ashurnasirpal wrote in a palace inscription that they ate "1,000 fattened head of cattle, 1,000 calves, 10,000 stable sheep, 15,000 lambs,... 500 stags, 500 gazelles, 1,000 ducks... 10,000 fish,... 10,000 eggs, 10,000 loaves of bread." Ashurnasirpal's guests would have left the party full of food, drink, and stories about the rich and powerful Assyrian king.

Ashurnasirpal II, royal inscription, ninth century BCE

LATER IN ROME...

In the first century CE, the Roman Empire grew even larger than the Assyrian Empire had been. It stretched east-west from Syria to Spain and north-south from Britain to southern Egypt. The Han dynasty, which flourished in China from 206 BCE to 220 CE, also controlled a great empire.

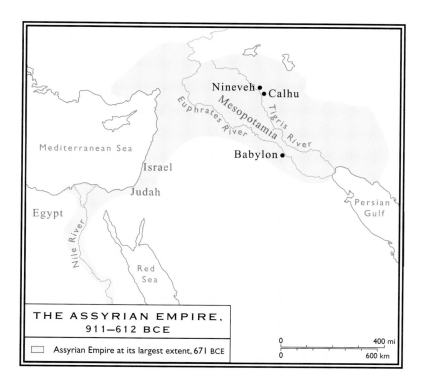

THE ASSYRIAN EMPIRE, 911–612 BCE

☐ Assyrian Empire at its largest extent, 671 BCE

0   400 mi
0   600 km

The kingdom of Assyria, located in the rolling hills in northern Mesopotamia, had existed since the second millennium BCE and had captured considerable power by 1300 BCE. And even though Assyria grew weak during the dark age that began around 1200 BCE, it never disappeared as a kingdom. By the 10th century BCE, the Assyrian kings began to dream of recapturing their former greatness. They attacked their neighbors and claimed that they were just taking back land that had once belonged to Assyria.

They believed it was a man's duty, and especially a king's duty, to be strong, brave, and warlike. When Ashurnasirpal II wasn't fighting, he liked to hunt dangerous lions and other wild animals.

During the 9th century, Assyrian kings gradually pushed beyond their old borders. They conquered many foreign peoples in order to take their gold, animals, timber, and other natural resources. Ashurnasirpal actually bragged in his royal inscriptions about his own cruelty: "I slaughtered great numbers of them [the inhabitants] . . . and carried off their possessions. I burned their cities with fire . . . and I imposed forced labor upon them."

Ashurnasirpal's reputation for brutality got around. Often after one city had been conquered, the others nearby just gave up without a fight. When this happened, the Assyrians sometimes rewarded them by letting the local king stay on his throne. This is what happened in Israel and Judah for many years. Their kings kept their jobs and handled local business, but they had to send much of their wealth to Assyria. According to an Assyrian inscription, King Jehu of Israel, for example, sent expensive tributes of "silver, gold, a golden bowl, . . . golden goblets, pitchers of gold, lead, [and] javelins."

During King Jehu's rule (around 842 to 815 BCE) Israel sent enough tribute money and gifts to keep the Assyrians from attacking, but later the Israelites rebelled. And in 722 BCE, the Assyrians crushed Israel. "Then the king of Assyria invaded all the land, . . . and for three years he besieged it [and] carried the Israelites away to Assyria." For the Assyrians, this was a minor victory. But for Israel, it was a

66 Ashurnasirpal II, royal inscription, 9th century BCE

66 Black obelisk, Iraq, 9th century BCE

66 II Kings, Hebrew Bible

King Jehu of Israel bows down to Shalmaneser III of Assyria, bringing tribute to him. Behind Jehu stand two Assyrians.

A ROYAL BOOKWORM

One of the last Assyrian kings, Ashurbanipal, was quite a different character from the earlier king Ashurnasirpal, even though their names are a lot alike. Ashurbanipal, who ruled from 668 to around 627 BCE, could read and write, and he loved to collect stories, which his scribes copied on cuneiform tablets. These tablet-books were arranged on shelves in Ashurbanipal's palace in Nineveh and included literature—some written long before Ashurbanipal's lifetime—from all over Mesopotamia. This was the world's first library. (To remember which king is which, think of the B that begins the word "book." The library-book king was Ashurbanipal.)

massive defeat. Their king was imprisoned, and countless Israelites were forced into exile. For the authors of the Hebrew Bible, who were from neighboring Judah, it was a turning point in history. They believed that God was punishing the Israelites for their sins.

At that point, the northern kingdom of Israel seems to disappear from history. Later authors called its people the 10 Lost Tribes of Israel. They weren't really lost, but the biblical authors stopped writing about them. Although many of the Israelites managed to stay on in their land, it seems that almost all the Israelites eventually gave up their worship of Yahweh—all except for the Israelites who lived in tiny Judah. But Judah, too, lived within the grip of Assyria's control.

Assyria managed to control its huge territory partly because it had such a well-organized system of government. The king didn't rule just by trusting his own instincts. He took advice from experts who formed a type of cabinet of advisers and scribes. And in each major city of the empire, a governor ruled in the king's place. These governors reported to the king. They collected taxes, drafted soldiers for the

Two Assyrian officials attend their king. Like most men at that time, they had pierced ears and wore large hoop earrings.

66 Sennacherib, royal inscription, 7th century BCE

army, and kept the roads safe for merchants and other travelers. The governors wrote to the king to keep him up-to-date about what was happening in their regions. The Assyrian kings kept the letters from their governors, as well as those from other advisers and family members. Archaeologists eventually found these letters at the palaces of the Assyrian kings.

During King Sennacherib's rule from 704 to 681 BCE, the Assyrian Empire was not only the biggest in the world, it was the biggest that had ever existed. Sennacherib's power stretched over a huge empire—about the size of modern Europe. But he was a brutal, cowardly man. He bragged in his inscriptions that he had savagely destroyed the beautiful city of Babylon. "I attacked it and, like a storm, I overthrew it...Its inhabitants, young and old, I did not spare. I filled the streets of the city with their corpses." This cruel king suffered a violent death himself—stabbed by one of his own sons.

King Sennacherib was not typical of Assyrian kings. Their methods worked so well that later rulers of other empires used many of Assyria's techniques: dividing the empire into provinces ruled by governors, stationing troops all over the empire, and controlling rebellions through swift military action. Even though the Assyrian Empire collapsed in the late seventh century, the spirit of its kings lived on in the rulers of the Roman Empire, who imitated their methods six centuries later.

CHAPTER 22

A BRIGHT STAR SHINES— BRIEFLY
BABYLON RISES, JUDAH FALLS

66 A BABYLONIAN CHRONICLE, A RATION LIST FROM BABYLON, THE SECOND BOOK OF KINGS, AND THE BOOK OF PSALMS

The Assyrian giant dominated the Near Eastern world for three centuries. But even at the height of its strength, the fierce Assyrians handled the kingdom of Babylon with **kid gloves**—much the way a younger brother might treat his talented, but moody, older sister. For example, when the Assyrian king Sennacherib destroyed Babylon, even the Assyrians saw it as a disaster. Sennacherib's son spent huge amounts rebuilding the city almost as soon as he took the throne. And the Assyrian kings agreed not to call up the Babylonians to do labor. They didn't want to be cursed by the Babylonian god, Marduk. A cuneiform document tells us that the Assyrian kings were afraid that if they "imposed forced labor on the people, . . . Marduk, prince of the gods . . .

Soft gloves made from the skin of a lamb or a baby goat. To treat someone "with kid gloves" means to use a gentle, delicate, or gingerly manner.

66 Cuneiform document, Iraq, 7th century BCE

A striding lion roars fiercely. He is one of the many creatures—real and imaginary—that decorate the glazed brick walls of Babylon's Processional Way.

BABYLON'S RISE

883–859 BCE
Ashurnasirpal II
of Assyria reigns

704–681 BCE
Sennacherib of Assyria
reigns

649–547 BCE
Adad-guppi, mother
of Nabonidus, lives

612 BCE
Nineveh is destroyed,
Assyrian Empire ends;
Neo-Babylonian
Empire begins

605–562 BCE
Nebuchadnezzar II
reigns

555–539 BCE
Nabonidus reigns

Neos = new, in Greek.
So Neo-Babylonian means
the new Babylonian Empire—
to distinguish it from the
Old Babylonian Empire of
Hammurabi, more than a
thousand years earlier.

would turn the land over to the enemy" and the Assyrians would wind up doing forced labor themselves.

In the middle of the seventh century, the whole Near East began to churn with rebellion. Power changed hands and thrones were lost as tribes and kingdoms battled against one another. During these years, even Assyria faced enemies who threatened to topple the giant from its perch of power. Its empire grew weak.

The Assyrians and the Babylonians were both Mesopotamian peoples and were related to one another. They spoke the same language, worshiped the same gods, and shared much of the same history. One of the powerful Assyrian kings had even taken the name Sargon in honor of the great Mesopotamian king who had lived almost 1,700 years before him in the region that became Babylon. And yet, despite all that they shared, the two peoples eventually fought.

The sword of power changed hands when the Babylonians and some of their allies conquered the much-weakened Assyria. By 612 BCE, Babylon controlled what was left of the Assyrian Empire. Assyria's three greatest cities had been destroyed—Ashur, home city of Assyria's most powerful god; Calhu, where Ashurnasirpal II had built his grand palace; and Nineveh with its magnificent buildings and the world's first library.

Nebuchadnezzar was the new "strong man" of the Near Eastern world. He probably had a long, curly beard, black hair to his shoulders, and he would have worn the long, embroidered robes and tall hat that proclaimed him a king. We have no pictures of him, but we can guess how he looked from the many images of other Mesopotamian kings since Sargon of Akkad. He was a warrior who spent most of his reign, from 605 to 562 BCE, leading his armies all across his empire, which stretched from Mesopotamia to Egypt. (Modern historians call Nebuchadnezzar's empire the **Neo-Babylonian** Empire.) But, like the Assyrian kings who ruled before him, Nebuchadnezzar had a lot of trouble with the kingdoms of the Levant. The Assyrians had already demolished the kingdom of Israel, but Judah was still alive and kicking against its foreign rulers.

King Jehoiachin came to Judah's throne when he was 18 years old. And that same winter, in March 597 BCE, Nebuchadnezzar attacked Jerusalem, Judah's capital. The Babylonian records describe the conquest in a matter-of-fact way:

> In the seventh year,...the king of Akkad [Nebuchadnezzar II] mustered his army and marched to Syria. He encamped against the city of Judah and on the second day of the month Adar [March 16, 597 BCE], he captured the city and seized its king. He appointed a [new] king...and brought a huge bounty to Babylon.

        66 Babylonian Chronicle, Iraq, 6th century BCE

A biblical writer describes the same battle in more detail because, for the people of Judah, the Babylonian victory was a disaster: "The officers of Nebuchadnezzar, king of Babylon, advanced on Jerusalem...and Nebuchadnezzar himself came up to the city while his officers were besieging it. Jehoiachin, king of Judah, his mother, his attendants, his nobles, and his officials all surrendered." According to the biblical record, Nebuchadnezzar's soldiers used their swords to cut in pieces all the golden treasures from the temple and from the king's house. They took the teenaged king captive, along with the whole royal family and 10,000 other Judeans. "Only the poorest people in the land were left" in Judah. The rest were exiled to Babylon.

        66 II Kings, Hebrew Bible

Nebuchadnezzar chose the next king of Judah—an Israelite who he thought would obey his commands. But this new king rebelled just nine years later, in 587 BCE. This time, the biblical writer reports that Nebuchadnezzar "marched against Jerusalem with his whole army" and besieged the capital for two years. "The famine in the city had become so serious that there was no food for the people to eat. Then the city wall was broken through, and the whole army [of Judah] fled at night through the gate." With its army gone, Judah was helpless. The Babylonians demolished Jerusalem, including the king's palace and Yahweh's temple.

When modern excavators dug up **Nebuchadnezzar's palace** in Babylon, they found documents listing rations that the government gave to various people. On the list of recipients were Judah's captured king and his family:

{ Nebuchadnezzar's palace was built later than Hammurabi's, so it's higher up—not waterlogged like the great lawgiver's palace, which lies below the water table.

66 Ration list, Iraq, 6th century
BCE

- 10 portions of oil to Jehoiakin the son of the king of Judah
- 2½ portions of oil for the five sons of the king of Judah

THE HANGING GARDENS OF... WHERE?

Centuries after Nebuchadnezzar's reign, Greeks and Romans praised what they called the Hanging Gardens of Babylon. The gardens probably didn't actually "hang." Most likely, they grew at the top of a building on artificial terraces. These lush, flourishing gardens high above the earth must have seemed like a miracle to ancient people.

There's only one problem: Nebuchadnezzar never mentioned the Hanging Gardens, and archaeologists have found no trace of them. But . . . there was exactly this type of terraced garden at the Assyrian capital of Nineveh. The Greeks and Romans were always confusing the Babylonians with the Assyrians. Perhaps they just got the city wrong— again. So the Hanging Gardens of Babylon, one of the Seven Wonders of the Ancient World, might really have been the Hanging Gardens of Nineveh.

Babylon was a huge and elaborate city in Nebuchadnezzar's time. The Euphrates flowed right through the middle of it, and a stone bridge connected the two halves of the city. A wide street, known as the Processional Way, led from Marduk's temple to a massive gate in the city wall, which was dedicated to the goddess Ishtar. The Processional Way and the Ishtar Gate were both decorated with bright blue, glazed bricks.

A Greek historian named Herodotus, writing a century

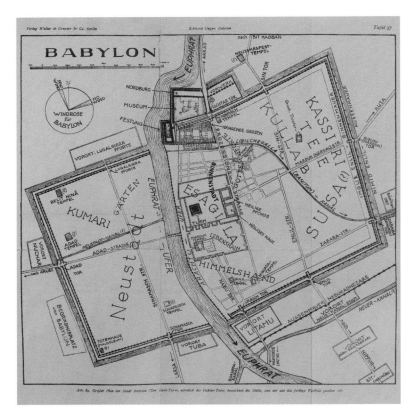

As this German archaeologist's map shows, Babylon was laid out as a huge rectangle, with major streets running north-south and east-west. The palace, Marduk's temple, and the Ishtar Gate were all in the city's eastern half.

later, wrote that even in decline, Babylon "surpasses in splendor any city of the known world." The king spent a lot of the empire's wealth building up the cities of Babylonia, especially Babylon itself. Excavations there have shown that the city covered three square miles, which was far bigger than most ancient cities in that time. Jerusalem, for example, was only about seven hundred yards across.

The **ziggurat**, a tall, terraced temple dedicated to the Babylonian god Marduk, dominated the skyline for miles around. It was built of baked bricks in seven huge steps, each step smaller than the one below it, with a staircase leading all the way from the ground to the shrine at the top. Unfortunately, none of its multicolored bricks have survived. They were all stolen or re-used in later buildings.

Ziggurat is our spelling of the Akkadian word *ziqquratu*, which means "temple tower" or sometimes "mountain peak." It comes from a verb *zaqaru*, which means "to build high."

The thousands of people deported from Judah must have been overwhelmed when they first came to Babylon. It was an international place that included people from all across the empire and beyond—people who spoke many different languages and who worshiped many different gods. The Israelites who came from Judah wrote songs, called Psalms, during their captivity in Babylon. Many of them show how much the exiles missed their home, especially Zion (another name for Jerusalem).

This modern painting of Babylon shows a city crowded with buildings and a grand street, known as the Processional Way, leading from the city's Ishtar Gate to Marduk's great temple. Ancient records and archaeological evidence agree that the Euphrates River flowed right through the middle of Babylon.

By the rivers of Babylon we sat and wept
when we remembered Zion
There on the poplars
we hung our harps,
for there our captors asked us for songs, . . .
[but] How can we sing the songs of the Lord
while in a foreign land?

❝ Psalms, Hebrew Bible

DANIEL IN THE LIONS' DEN

In the second century BCE, long after Nebuchadnezzar's reign, a Jewish author wrote the Book of Daniel. This biblical story, set in Nebuchadnezzar's time, centers on an Israelite named Daniel, who lived in Babylon. Daniel had a gift for interpreting dreams, which both the Israelites and the Babylonians believed could carry messages from God or the gods. Daniel even interpreted King Nebuchadnezzar's dreams. Some of the king's advisers were jealous of Daniel's influence with the king. So they tricked the king into passing a law that would have kept Daniel from worshipping Yahweh for 30 days. When Daniel was caught praying, he was thrown into a den of hungry lions. Daniel's enemies thought that they had won—but Daniel escaped without a scratch. Daniel explained to the king, "my God sent his angel and shut the lions' mouths, and they have not hurt me."

When Nebuchadnezzar built the dramatic Ishtar Gate into Babylon, he commanded his artists to cover its glazed surface with colorful sculptures, proclaiming the greatness of Babylon and its god Marduk.

The Israelites, whom we now call Jews because they were the people of Judah, may have thought that they'd never return to Judah. At times, they might have been tempted, like the 10 Lost Tribes of Israel, to give up their worship of Yahweh, to sigh in defeat, and worship Marduk instead. But they didn't give up their beliefs. Instead, during their exile in Babylon, new prophets arose telling them that Yahweh loved them and had forgiven them. These prophets told them that their God was the only god—that the Babylonians' gods were just pieces of wood. Jewish writers and editors began to collect, arrange, and edit the books of the Hebrew Bible. Perhaps they wanted to make sure the people would remember their stories.

In spite of the sad tone of the psalms, the Jews seem to have adjusted to life in Babylon and even prospered there. When they eventually got the chance to return to Judah, decades later, some returned. But many chose to stay in Babylon. And today, in Iraq, there are still a few Jews who say that their families have lived there for more than 2,500 years.

CHAPTER 23

A MOTHER'S LOVE AND A RULER'S TEARS

THE LAST MESOPOTAMIAN KING

E ven as a child, Adad-Guppi was devoted to the gods. She explained, in her autobiography carved on two paving stones, that she was "a servant of Sin, Ningal, Nusku, and Sadarnunna, my gods, for whose divinity I have cared since my youth." She served all four gods, but the moon god Sin was the one she loved best.

❝ Adad-Guppi, autobiography, 547 BCE

Adad-Guppi was 37 years old when the Babylonians conquered the Assyrian Empire in 612 BCE. She lived in the Assyrian city of Harran, where she was a priestess in the temple of Sin. Even though the Babylonian victory was a major public event, it probably didn't affect her daily life very much. The Babylonians ran the empire pretty much the way the Assyrians had done. People still had to eat, sleep, and pay taxes. And the gods still needed her care and attention.

But in 610 BCE, something terrible happened. Adad-Guppi put it this way: "Sin, the king of all gods, became angry with his city [Harran] . . . and went up to heaven, and the city and the people in it became desolate." Exactly what happened in Harran is a mystery because archaeologists haven't done much excavating there. But we know from inscriptions from other places that Harran was conquered by one of Babylon's allies, who captured the statue of the god Sin. Adad-Guppi was heartbroken. The temple in which she had worked and worshiped was destroyed. The

An ancient craftsman carved this scepter out of a fine, striped stone known as onyx. The king would have handed a scepter like this one to the priest during the Babylonian New Year's festival.

god she loved was gone. Adad-Guppi became obsessed with her wish to bring Sin back to Harran. She also wanted to rebuild the temple, but that would cost a fortune. She knew she couldn't do these things all by herself.

Adad-Guppi had to wait throughout Nebuchadnezzar's long reign before her dreams came true. Nebuchadnezzar spent huge amounts of money on Babylon, while almost ignoring Harran. Luckily, the priestess was a patient woman. She waited and prayed for 54 years. Then in 555 BCE, when Adad-Guppi was in her 90s, her long wait ended. In a surprising twist of fortune, her adored son, Nabonidus, became king of the Neo-Babylonian Empire. How did this happen? He wasn't from the royal family. For his mother, the reason was obvious: Sin had answered her prayers. She had a scribe write in her autobiography:

❝ Adad-Guppi, autobiography, 547 BCE

> Sin, the king of all the gods, looked with favor upon me and called Nabonidus, my only son, whom I bore, to kingship and entrusted him with the kingship of Sumer and Akkad, also of all the countries from the border of Egypt, on the Upper Sea, to the Lower Sea.

After Nebuchadnezzar's death, three men claimed the throne in turn, and each one ruled for a year or two. Nabonidus was the fourth man to become king of Babylon in just six years, and he may have murdered King Number 3. But to Adad-Guppi, his kingship was a gift—not from the Babylonian god Marduk, but from Sin.

❝ Adad-Guppi, autobiography, 547 BCE

Soon after Nabonidus took the throne, his mother dreamed that "Sin, the king of all the gods, . . . said: 'The gods will return because of you. I will entrust your son, Nabonidus, with the divine residence of Harran; he will rebuild the temple.'" When a god appeared in a dream, the Mesopotamians believed that the god was sending a message to the dreamer. So when Nabonidus had a similar dream, he began rebuilding the temple in Harran.

Adad-Guppi lived to see her son rule for nine years. It must have given her great joy to see Sin's temple rebuilt. She claimed that she had lived to be 104 years old, an almost unheard-of great age in those days. (In fact, she seems to

A priest stands, in a gesture of prayer, before symbols of the gods Marduk and Nabu. This blue clay seal was made during the Neo-Babylonian period.

have died at 102 or 103.) Nabonidus invited governors and princes from all over the empire to attend his mother's funeral. He described these events in a P.S. to his mother's autobiography. The visitors mourned for seven days, "their heads hung low, dust strewn" after which Nabonidus bought them all new clothes, "treated them with food and drink,... poured scented oil over their heads, made them glad again" before sending them home.

Nabonidus was not typical of Mesopotamian kings. For one thing, he rarely lived in Babylonia, the land that he ruled. In an inscription carved on stone slabs in his mother's city of Harran, he blames the god Sin for this: "He made me leave... Babylon.... For 10 years, I... did not enter my own city." Kings were expected to live in their capital cities. In Mesopotamia, this was especially important because of the New Year's Festival held in Babylon each year. The Mesopotamians, like people in many ancient societies, celebrated the new year at the beginning of spring. They believed that the city's prosperity and, in fact, the safety of the entire universe depended upon this ritual. And the king played the leading role in this yearly drama.

The New Year's Festival took place in Marduk's temple. For four days, the priests sang hymns and performed rituals to free the temple of all impurities. On the fifth day, the king and a high priest were called into the room where Marduk's statue was kept. This was a very holy place, dark and quiet, scented with incense, with the gold of the god's statue glinting in the light from their oil lamps. Once inside, the high priest took away the king's scepter, crown, and sword and slapped him on the cheek. Next the priest was supposed to drag the king

❝ Nabonidus, royal inscription, around 542 BCE

“ Temple Program for the New Year's Festival, Babylon, 3rd to 1st century BCE

MEANWHILE IN EGYPT...

Like the Mesopotamians, the ancient Egyptians honored their dead by a long period of mourning. When members of the Egyptian royal family died, their bodies were mummified. The process took about six weeks. First, the internal organs were removed and preserved—all except the brain. It was cut into pieces, which were pulled out through the nose and thrown away. After that, the body was packed in salt for 40 days to completely dry out. Then it was wrapped in linen strips, with magical charms and jewels placed inside the bandages. A mask that represented the dead person was placed over the mummy's face, and the mummy was placed inside a stone coffin. And then, like the Babylonians of Nabonidus's time, the Egyptians held a great feast to honor the dead.

by the ears and make him bow down to the ground.... The king shall say [to Marduk] ... "I did not sin, lord of the countries. I did not neglect the requirements of your godship.... I watched out for Babylon; I did not smash its walls."

After this humble speech by the king, the high priest returned the symbols of his royal power. But then he slapped the king's face again—hard. According to the "script," if "the tears flow, it means that the god ... is friendly, but if no tears appear, the god ... is angry." A king's dry eyes meant that his enemies would soon defeat him. (It's likely that most kings had the good sense to cry.)

Why would a king allow himself to be treated as though he were less important than the high priest? The ritual made sense only if the king actually believed that he was saving his people and the world from chaos, that his show of humility truly made Marduk happy. Once the yearly ritual had assured the people that Marduk would protect them in the year ahead, the parades and parties began.

When Nebuchadnezzar was king, he played his part in the New Year's Festival. He probably believed that it worked. But Nabonidus, like his mother, honored the moon god,

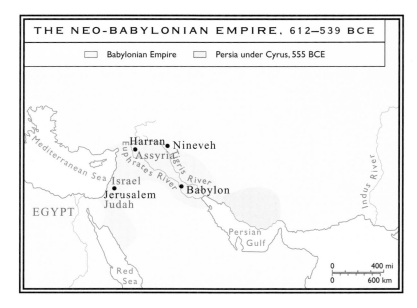

THE NEO-BABYLONIAN EMPIRE, 612–539 BCE

☐ Babylonian Empire ☐ Persia under Cyrus, 555 BCE

and was much less interested in Marduk. Was that why he stayed away from Babylon for so long?

By the time Nabonidus finally returned to Babylon in 542 BCE, his people must have hated him. The festival had been cancelled for 10 years. He had risked the peace and prosperity of the entire world—was he a madman? Nabonidus probably wasn't crazy, but his terrible reputation in Babylon suited one person very well: King Cyrus of Persia.

Early in his reign in Persia, in the highlands to the east of Mesopotamia, Cyrus began a propaganda campaign against Nabonidus. He wrote inscriptions claiming that Marduk was unhappy with Nabonidus and wanted Cyrus to rule over Babylonia. Cyrus promised that he would return Marduk to his rightful place as king of the gods.

In fact, Cyrus probably wasn't much interested in Marduk. He honored his own Persian god above all others. But he made a convincing case. No one knows what the Babylonians actually thought about Cyrus. Maybe they fell for his promises, maybe not. Cyrus claimed in an inscription carved on a barrel-shaped tablet that "All the inhabitants of Babylon as well as of the entire country of Sumer and Akkad, princes and governors included, bowed to Cyrus and kissed his feet, jubilant . . . with shining faces." In Cyrus's version of the story he was welcomed with open arms. Other records tell us that, in 539 BCE, Cyrus had to fight a battle before he could take power in Babylonia. So maybe the Babylonians *didn't* rush to kiss his feet.

Near Eastern history might have been different if Nabonidus had been more interested in the beliefs of his people. But Cyrus wasn't much better than Nabonidus. Despite his claims, he had no intention of living in Mesopotamia. He lived in Persia. After defeating the Babylonians, Mesopotamia became just one of his provinces, ruled by a governor. And Nabonidus? He survived, but in exile. Was he glad that his mother didn't live to see the sad end to his promising reign?

The dragon was the symbol of the god Marduk. This molded brick serpent-like dragon decorates the Ishtar gate in Babylon.

"Cyrus Cylinder," inscription, around 539 BCE

CHAPTER 24

OF CAMELS, KINGS, AND CONQUERORS
THE PERSIAN EMPIRE

" A GREEK HISTORY, A PERSIAN KING'S INSCRIPTION, AND THE BOOK OF ISAIAH

Croesus ruled the land of Lydia, far to the north and west of Mesopotamia. When the Persian army under King Cyrus attacked Lydia, Croesus was confident that his troops would defeat them. But he was wrong—almost dead wrong! One problem was that the Persians rode camels into battle, and their camels terrified the Lydians' horses. The Greek historian Herodotus wrote that the Lydians were losing badly, and an ordinary Persian soldier almost killed Croesus, not realizing that he was the king.

" Herodotus, *Histories*, 5th century BCE

> Croesus saw him coming; but because in his misery he did not care if he lived or died, he made no effort to defend himself. But [his] mute son, seeing the danger, was so terrified . . . that he broke into speech, and cried: "Do not kill Croesus, fellow!" Those were the first words he ever uttered—and he kept the power of speech for the rest of his life.

Croesus was taken to King Cyrus, who commanded that the enemy king be burned alive. Attendants prepared the firewood, placed Croesus on the top, and lit the edges of the woodpile. The flames were coming dangerously near, but Croesus prayed to the gods for rescue. Herodotus wrote: "It was a clear and windless day; but suddenly in answer to Croesus's prayer, clouds gathered and a storm broke with such violent rain that the flames were put out." According to Herodotus, these two miracles convinced Cyrus that the gods wanted Croesus to live. The Persian king appointed Croesus as one of his trusted advisers. That was Herodotus's story, anyway, but he loved to tell tall tales. There are no accounts by the Lydians or the Persians to back them up.

Whether or not this story is true, we know that Croesus

LATER IN ITALY...

About 350 years after Cyrus's camels frightened the Lydians' horses, another general staged a similar victory. This later general was the North African leader Hannibal, whose war elephants—with their trunks painted red—frightened the Roman horses and helped Hannibal to defeat the most powerful army of his day.

and Cyrus were real kings. From 560 to 547 BCE, Croesus ruled the kingdom of Lydia, a beautiful land near the Mediterranean, with green hills and orchards, threaded through with small rivers and streams.

Cyrus's kingdom centered in what is now Iran, on a high plateau in the Zagros Mountains, almost two thousand miles from Croesus's land. In 550 BCE, in the ninth year of his reign, Cyrus conquered a neighboring people known as the Medes, whose kingdom stretched from Anatolia through Assyria to the Oxus River. So, when Cyrus overcame the Medes, he became the ruler of a huge empire, with Lydia just beyond its western border.

Cyrus was determined to expand his empire. His triumph over Croesus was his second

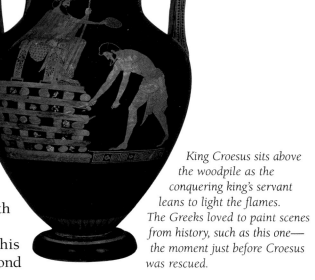

King Croesus sits above the woodpile as the conquering king's servant leans to light the flames. The Greeks loved to paint scenes from history, such as this one—the moment just before Croesus was rescued.

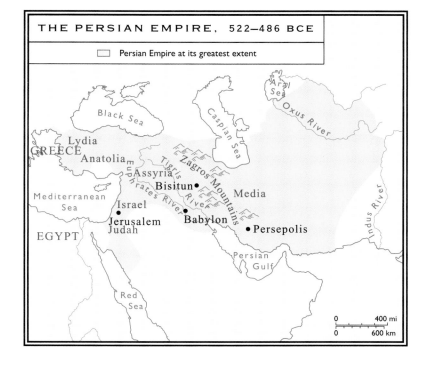

THE PERSIAN EMPIRE, 522–486 BCE

☐ Persian Empire at its greatest extent

major victory, and others soon followed. Nabonidus, the unpopular king of the Neo-Babylonian Empire, was another target of Cyrus's ambition. Cyrus had a royal inscription carved on a barrel-shaped tablet to celebrate his easy victory over Babylon. In the inscription, he described himself in much the same way that Mesopotamian kings had done ever since the earliest Sumerian city-states, almost 2,500 years earlier:

66 "Cyrus Cylinder," inscription, around 539 BCE

I am Cyrus, king of the world, . . . rightful king . . . of Babylon, king of Sumer and Akkad, king of the four rims (of the earth), . . . king of Anshan [Persia] . . . of a family (that) always ruled; whose reign Bel [Marduk] . . . love(s).

Even though he conquered an empire, Cyrus, like Hammurabi, boasted in the same inscription: "I did not allow anybody to terrorize any place in the country of Sumer and Akkad. I aimed for peace in Babylon and in all [Marduk's] other cities." He described his generosity to other cities: "I brought relief to their broken-down housing." He claimed that all the gods loved him: "I resettled . . . all the gods of Sumer and Akkad . . . in their former chapels—the places which make them happy."

Many in the empire agreed with Cyrus's high opinion of himself. Some of the Jews in Babylon even considered him to be Yahweh's "anointed," the chosen one, because he allowed them to return to Jerusalem and helped them to rebuild their temple. One biblical prophet, Isaiah, wrote as though Yahweh himself was speaking: "I am the Lord, who has made all things . . . who says of Cyrus, 'He is my shepherd and will accomplish all that I please; he will say of Jerusalem, 'Let it be rebuilt,' and of the temple, 'Let its foundation be laid.'"

66 Isaiah, Hebrew Bible

After Cyrus's death, two kings ruled the Persian Empire, each for a very short time. Then Darius took the throne. (He probably overthrew Cyrus's son.) Darius, who ruled from 522 to 486 BCE, wanted to be remembered as one of the greatest kings of all time. So he had an inscription carved high on a mountainside at a place called Bisitun to celebrate the glories of his reign. An image of Darius himself topped the inscription, which was carved in three languages. The king commanded that the stone around the inscription should be smooth and polished so that no one could climb up and deface his name or erase the record of his accomplishments. And it worked—the inscription still proclaims Darius's achievements, just as he hoped it would.

What Darius couldn't have known is that his mountainside inscription would become the key that opened the languages of his day. He wrote the same message in Persian, Akkadian, and Elamite—the language spoken in Elam, Mesopotamia's neighbor and long-time enemy. Because all three of these languages were written in cuneiform scripts, scholars have used Darius's inscription to decipher these ancient languages.

Darius's inscriptions show that he worshiped the god Ahura Mazda. The king gave Ahura Mazda credit for all his military victories and praised him as the creator of the universe and the god of justice, goodness, and virtue. Darius seems to have believed that the gods of other peoples were just different names for Ahura Mazda. The Babylonians

AS RICH AS CROESUS

The Greeks described Lydia, their neighbor to the east across the Aegean Sea, as a tremendously rich country and its king Croesus as wealthy beyond belief. In fact, the burial mounds of the Lydian kings were the largest and among the wealthiest in Anatolia.

A victorious King Darius speaks to his captured enemies beneath the image of the god Ahura Mazda. Workers carved this scene and its inscription high up on a rock face at Bisitun.

MAPPING HEAVEN

The Zoroastrians of Persia believed in a peaceful, heavenly existence after death for those who had lived good lives. This was unusual among Near Eastern peoples at this time. The Egyptians were the only others who believed in such a heaven. They even made maps showing where its rivers and towns were located.

"Satrap" comes from the Old Persian word *shathrapavan*, which means "protector of the land." }

might worship Marduk, for instance, or the Greeks might worship Zeus, but they were all actually worshiping Ahura Mazda. The Persian kings never forced their subjects to change their religion—everyone was worshiping one god anyway, just using different names for him.

An influential Persian teacher named Zoroaster, who had lived before the reigns of Cyrus and Darius (it's unclear exactly when), preached about Ahura Mazda. Zoroaster taught that this god constantly fought against a demon called The Lie. He explained that each person was responsible to choose good over evil and that all of history was a tale of human beings acting out the struggle between Ahura Mazda and The Lie. Zoroastrians tried to live good lives in order to please Ahura Mazda. They believed that eventually Ahura Mazda would win out over The Lie.

Darius's inscriptions never mention Zoroaster's name, but his beliefs mirror the prophet's teachings. Darius wanted to be a good ruler, but he also longed to be a glorious one. His capital city at Persepolis set a new standard for grandeur. Many of the buildings and sculptures can still be seen there today, towering over the surrounding plateau in what is now Iran. Darius brought in architects and sculptors from many regions to create the art for his capital. He had images of people from all the different parts of his empire carved onto the walls, in endless processions, bringing tribute to him.

During Darius's reign, the Persian Empire became the biggest the world had ever known. It stretched from South Asia all the way to western Anatolia and into Egypt. Darius divided his empire into 20 provinces and appointed a governor, known as a **satrap**, to handle local business, maintain justice, and keep peace in each province. But despite his ambition and his many victories, Darius met a stinging defeat in 490 BCE when the Greeks crushed the army he had sent to conquer them. Greece was just a collection of independent city-states. It was tiny, compared to the great, unified Persian Empire. Victory over them should have been a cinch, but it wasn't.

Ten years later, Darius's son Xerxes tried to avenge

Persia's shameful defeat and bring Greece into the Persian Empire. But even though the Persian army was huge, the Greeks won again. The Greeks saw this victory as so earth-shaking that Herodotus wrote the very first history book to celebrate the events of this war and the victory of the heroic Greeks over the mighty Persians.

Although Mesopotamia was now a province, not an independent kingdom, life there under Persian rule doesn't seem to have changed very much from life under Babylonian or Assyrian kings. In fact, life hadn't changed much for 1,200 years. Marduk's temple in Babylon was still in the same place. Judges still heard court cases. Scribes still wrote in the Akkadian language on clay tablets. Houses looked almost the same, and people farmed in much the same way they always had. But the picture was about to change dramatically.

Once again, the Greeks staged a surprising victory, this time led by an ambitious conqueror, Alexander the Great who came to power when he was only 19 years old. In 330

King Darius's palace at Persepolis was built on a high platform with a fabulous view of the surrounding countryside. Some of the huge columns that once held up the ceiling are still standing.

THE PERSIAN EMPIRE

560–547 BCE
Croesus of Lydia reigns

559–530 BCE
Cyrus of Persia reigns

550 BCE
Cyrus defeats Medes; Persian Empire founded

547 BCE
Cyrus defeats Lydia

539 BCE
Cyrus defeats Neo-Babylonian Empire

522–486 BCE
Darius I of Persia reigns

490 BCE
Persia attacks Greece

486–465 BCE
Xerxes of Persia reigns

330 BCE
Alexander the Great defeats Persian Empire

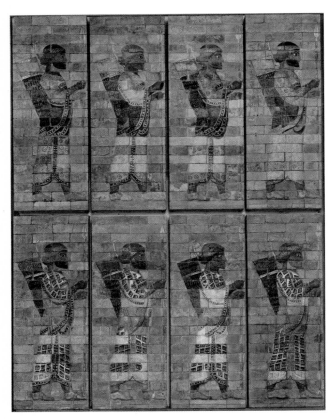

Life-sized archers line the walls of Darius's palace. The Persians learned from the Babylonians how to create sculptures using glazed bricks.

BCE, the Greeks, under Alexander, crushed the Persian Empire finally and completely, defeating its last king. The end of the Persian Empire also marked the end of a culture.

Alexander took the clay of the ancient Near East and reshaped it into a very different world. He and the kings who followed him established Greek as the official language of the empire. Even local Babylonians had to learn Greek if they wanted to get ahead. Gradually people forgot the ancient languages of Akkadian and Sumerian. Only a few well-educated scribes could still read cuneiform. And people began to forget the stories that had thrilled them for centuries: stories of the creator god Enlil or the hero Gilgamesh or the mighty king Sargon.

The Greeks built new cities in their own style, with market places, theaters, and gymnasiums. Lavish temples honoring Greek gods, such as Zeus and Athena, dominated the city centers. Meanwhile, the ancient Near Eastern gods—Shamash, Marduk, Ishtar, and all the others—were neglected and eventually abandoned. The Greeks learned astronomy, mathematics, military strategies, and many other things from the Mesopotamians. The concepts of law developed by the Mesopotamians survived, as did the religions of the Jews and the Zoroastrians. But after a few centuries of Greek rule, most of the ancient Near Eastern languages, religions, writing systems, and governments were all lost. The world of the ancient Mesopotamians had disappeared.

EPILOGUE
A WORLD NOT TRULY LOST

The ancient Near East was home to one of the longest lasting, most successful civilizations the world has ever seen. Imagine a timeline stretching from the time of the first cities to the present—about 5,500 years. Mesopotamian civilization flourished for more than half of those years: from around 3500 to 330 BCE . . . more than three thousand years. In contrast, the first towns in what later became the United States were founded in the early 1600s, less than four hundred years ago.

During those three millennia of Mesopotamia's existence, the people made countless inventions that changed the world. They rightly saw themselves at the cutting edge of science and technology. They devised one of the world's first writing systems and the first law collection. The first cities and the first empires grew in these lands. These imaginative people invented the wheel, plow, boat, and irrigation canal—to name just a few more of Mesopotamia's "firsts."

Babylonian architects built vast, stable, brick structures, such as ziggurats and city walls. Mesopotamia's astronomers could predict eclipses of the sun and the moon, and its mathematicians figured out what we call the Pythagorean Theorem (the formula used to calculate the length of one side of a right triangle) more than a thousand years before the Greek mathematician Pythagorus rediscovered it.

A Mesopotamian scribe wrote about right triangles on this tablet. He used the Pythagorean Theorem, which says that in a right-angle triangle where a and b are the two shorter sides and c is the long side, $a^2 + b^2 = c^2$.

On one side of a coin, seafaring Phoenicians sail above a fantastic sea creature with a horse's head and a fish's tail. Coins, invented by the Lydians, became popular among ancient peoples all across the Near East and the Mediterranean.

By the time King Cyrus conquered Mesopotamia, irrigation agriculture made it the wealthiest land in the Persian Empire. Its complicated system of canals, levees, and reservoirs kept the rivers under control and prevented serious floods for hundreds of years. Mesopotamia's neighbors also left important legacies, such as the alphabet from Canaan and money from Lydia. The Phoenicians, in the Levant, mastered boat building and sea navigation and spread their alphabet to other lands.

The people of the ancient Near East are important not only for these world-changing inventions, but also for their ideas and values. Some of the very first royal inscriptions were designed to keep strong or rich people from taking advantage of the poor. The Mesopotamian legal system aimed to prevent corruption, promote fairness, and foster justice. These ancient peoples seem to have lived without much fear of crime and without much fear of the law itself. We know of very few instances where death penalties were actually carried out. Most criminals just paid fines for their offenses.

The people of the ancient Near East expected good behavior of themselves and each another. Someone who cared for his family, dealt fairly with others, and obeyed the laws could hope that the gods would reward him or her with a long life and good luck. One Mesopotamian proverb summed up these expectations, "Commit no crime, and fear of your god will not consume you. Speak no wrong and then grief will not reach your heart. Do no evil and then you will not experience lasting misfortune." The Mesopotamians had a lot of proverbs to help them live a good life. Another proverb, a version of the Golden Rule, tells a newly married woman "Bride, as you treat your mother-in-law, so will women later treat you."

One of the most influential ideas to develop in the ancient Near East was monotheism, an idea that spread gradually at first but came to be adopted by many of the world's peoples.

In the centuries after Alexander the Great of Greece conquered his empire, people forgot that the Mesopotamians and other peoples of the Near East had developed all these ideas. Some mentions of the Assyrians in the Hebrew Bible and in the writings of Herodotus described the great civilizations that had once existed in the Near East. But by the beginning of modern times, few people realized how ancient or how brilliant these cultures had been. Historians gave credit to the Greeks for many ideas and inventions that had actually come from the peoples of the ancient Near East.

During the 19th century, language experts deciphered cuneiform and archaeologists began to dig in Iraq, Iran, Syria, and Turkey—and they began to uncover ancient secrets. Like multiple Alices tumbling down the rabbit hole, archaeologists rediscovered a hidden world that once had been peopled with kings and queens, heroes and common folk. The dreams, ambitions, hopes, fears, and feelings of these people came alive through the texts that they wrote and the remnants that they left of their lives.

MANY SHADES OF GOLD

Some version of the Golden Rule appears in the writings of nearly every religion. The Christian New Testament's Book of Matthew says: "Whatever you wish that men would do to you, do so to them." The Hadith of the Muslims warns: "No one of you is a believer until he desires for his brother that which he desires for himself." The Mahabharata of the Hindus advises: "Do nothing to others which, if done to you, would cause you pain." The Jewish Talmud says: "What is hateful to you, do not do to your fellow men." And the Udana-Varga of the Buddhists puts it this way: "Hurt not others with that which pains yourself." The message is the same.

TIMELINE

The centuries BCE and CE are mirror images of each other. The years go backwards before the Year 1 CE. So someone born in 2000 BCE who died in 1935 BCE would have lived to be 65 years old. On both sides of the "mirror," the 200s can also be called the 3rd century, the 900s are called the 10th century and so on—BCE as well as CE.

8000–3800 BCE
Neolithic Age

8000 BCE
First farming communities in the Near East; tokens first used as accounting system

5000 BCE
Southern Mesopotamia first settled; first shrine built at Eridu

4000 BCE
First towns established in Mesopotamia and Syria

3800–1200 BCE
Bronze Age

3800–3100 BCE
Uruk period

3500 BCE
Cities develop in Mesopotamia; pottery wheel first used; plow invented

3350 BCE
Accounting tokens enclosed in clay balls

3200 BCE
Pictographic writing invented

3100 BCE
Wheel and first wagon invented

3000 BCE
Use of cuneiform writing begins

2900 BCE
Kingship and city-states begin

2600–2450 BCE
Royal tombs of Ur built

2600 BCE
Mebaragesi writes first-known royal inscription; Gilgamesh of Uruk possibly reigns

around 2500 BCE
Indo-Europeans begin to migrate

2400 BCE
Eannatum of Lagash reigns; city of Ebla flourishes in Syria; first personal letters written

2340–2284 BCE
Sargon of Akkad reigns and creates first empire, installs daughter Enheduanna as high priestess

around 2300 BCE
Ebla destroyed

2300 BCE
Burials at Umm el-Marra

2260–2223 BCE
Naram-Sin of Akkad reigns

2113–2096 BCE
Ur-Namma of Ur reigns

2094–2047 BCE
Reign of Shulgi of Ur, creator of first law
collection

around 2000 BCE
Amorites invade Mesopotamia

2000–1500
Old Babylonian Period

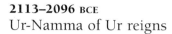

1792–1750 BCE
Hammurabi of
Babylon reigns

1775–1761 BCE
Zimri-Lim of Mari
reigns

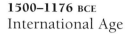

1755 BCE
Hammurabi's laws
established

1749–1712 BCE
Samsu-iluna of Babylon reigns

1650 BCE
Sippar destroyed

1625–1595 BCE
Samsu-ditana of Babylon reigns

1595 BCE
Mursili I of Hatti attacks Babylon;
Old Babylonian Empire ends

1595–1500 BCE
Period of turmoil in the Near East

1500–1176 BCE
International Age

1500 BCE
Kassites in power
in Babylon;
Kingdom of Mittani
begins; Hittite
Empire expands

1387–1350 BCE
Amenhotep III reigns in Egypt; height
of the International Age

around 1200 BCE
Sin-leqe-unnini writes *Epic of Gilgamesh*

around 1200 BCE
Jews arrive in the Levant

1185 BCE
Ugarit, Syria, and Hattusa, Hittite capital,
destroyed

1176 BCE
Sea Peoples attack Egypt

1200 BCE
Iron Age begins

1176–911 BCE
Dark Age

around 1020 BCE
Saul of Israel reigns

around 1000 BCE
David of Israel reigns

around 960 BCE
Solomon of Israel reigns

922 BCE
Israel divides into two kingdoms

911–612
Assyrian Empire

885–874 BCE
Omri of Israel reigns

883–859 BCE
Ashurnasirpal II of Assyria reigns

722 BCE
Assyria conquers Israel

704–681 BCE
Sennacherib of Assyria reigns

649–547 BCE
Adad-guppi, mother of Nabonidus, lives

612 BCE
Nineveh destroyed; Assyrian Empire ends

612 BCE
Neo-Babylonian Empire begins

605–562 BCE
Nebuchadnezzar of Babylon reigns

598–597 BCE
Jehoiakin of Judah reigns

587 BCE
Babylon conquers Judah

560–547 BCE
Croesus of Lydia reigns

559–530 BCE
King Cyrus of Persia reigns

555–539 BCE
Nabonidus of the Neo-Babylonian Empire reigns

550 BCE
Cyrus defeats the Medes; founds Persian Empire

547 BCE
Cyrus defeats Lydia

539 BCE
Cyrus conquers Neo-Babylonian Empire

522–486 BCE
Darius I of Persia reigns

490 BCE
Persia attacks Greece

486–465 BCE
Xerxes of Persia reigns

330 BCE
Alexander the Great defeats the Persian Empire

FURTHER READING

Entries with 🔲 *indicate primary source material.*

GENERAL WORKS

🔲 Foster, Benjamin R. *Before the Muses: An Anthology of Akkadian Literature.* 2nd ed. Bethesda, Md.: CDL Press, 1996.

Malam, John. *Mesopotamia and the Fertile Crescent.* Austin, Tex.: Steck-Vaughn, 1999.

Mesopotamia Issue. *Calliope: World History Magazine for Young People* 4, no. 1 (September/October 1993).

Oakes, Lorna. *Step Into... Mesopotamia.* New York: Lorenz, 2001.

Oppenheim, A. Leo. *Ancient Mesopotamia: Portrait of a Dead Civilization.* Rev. ed. Edited by Erica Reiner. Chicago: University of Chicago Press, 1977.

🔲 Pritchard, James B., ed. *Ancient Near Eastern Texts.* 3rd ed. Princeton, N.J.: Princeton University Press, 1969.

Roux, Georges. *Ancient Iraq.* 3rd ed. New York: Penguin, 1992.

ATLASES

Haywood, John. *World Atlas of the Past.* Vol. 1, *The Ancient World: Earliest Times to 1 BC.* New York: Oxford University Press, 1999.

Hunter, Erica C. D., with updates by Mike Corbishley. *Cultural Atlas for Young People: First Civilizations.* Rev. ed. New York: Facts on File, 2003.

Roaf, Michael. *Cultural Atlas of Mesopotamia and the Ancient Near East.* New York: Facts on File, 1990.

DICTIONARIES AND ENCYCLOPEDIAS

Wallenfels, Ronald, and Jack M. Sasson, eds. *The Ancient Near East: An Encyclopedia for Students.* New York: Scribner, 2000.

BIOGRAPHY

Leick, Gwendolyn. *Who's Who in the Ancient Near East.* New York: Routledge, 1999.

ARCHAEOLOGY

Meyers, Eric M., ed. *The Oxford Encyclopedia of Archaeology in the Near East.* New York: Oxford University Press, 1997.

Weiss, Harvey, ed. *Ebla to Damascus: Art and Archaeology of Ancient Syria.* Washington, D.C.: Smithsonian Institution Traveling Exhibition Service, 1985.

Woolley, Leonard, Sir. *Ur "of the Chaldees": A Revised and Updated Edition of Sir Leonard Woolley's Excavations at Ur.* Rev., updated ed. Edited by P. R. S. Moorey. Ithaca, N.Y.: Cornell University Press, 1982.

ART AND ARCHITECTURE

Aruz, Joan, ed., with Ronald Wallenfels. *Art of the First Cities: The Third Millennium B.C. from the Mediterranean to the Indus.* New Haven, Conn.: Yale University Press, 2003.

Leacock, Helen, and Richard Leacock. *The Buildings of Ancient Mesopotamia.* Reading, Mass.: Addison-Wesley, 1974.

ASSYRIANS

🔲 Grayson, Albert K. *Assyrian and Babylonian Chronicles.* Locust Valley, N.Y.: J. J. Augustin, 1975.

Landau, Elaine. *The Assyrians.* Brookfield, Conn.: Millbrook Press, 1997.

BABYLONIANS

Foster, P. "The Earliest Zoos and Gardens." *Scientific American,* July 1999.

[66] Grayson, Albert K. *Assyrian and Babylonian Chronicles.* Locust Valley, N.Y.: J. J. Augustin, 1975.

Landau, Elaine. *The Babylonians.* Brookfield, Conn.: Millbrook Press, 1997.

CITIES

Stone, E., and P. Zimansky, "The Tapestry of Power in a Mesopotamian City." *Scientific American,* April 1995.

Wilkinson, Philip and Jacqueline Dineen. *Mysterious Places: The Lands of the Bible.* New York: Chelsea House, 1994.

Van de Mieroop, Marc. *The Ancient Mesopotamian City.* New York: Oxford University Press, 1997.

DAILY LIFE

Bottéro, Jean. *Everyday Life in Ancient Mesopotamia.* Baltimore, Md.: John Hopkins University Press, 2001.

Nemet-Nejat, Karen R. *Daily Life in Ancient Mesopotamia.* Peabody, Mass.: Hendrickson Publishers, 2002.

[66] Oppenheim, A. Leo. *Letters from Mesopotamia.* Chicago: University of Chicago Press, 1967.

Podany, Amanda H., ed. Children of Ancient Mesopotamia Issue. *AppleSeeds* (October 2004).

Snell, Daniel C. *Life in the Ancient Near East, 3100–332 B.C.E.* New Haven, Conn.: Yale University Press, 1997.

LAW AND GOVERNMENT

[66] Moran, William L. *The Amarna Letters.* Baltimore, Md.: Johns Hopkins University Press, 1992.

[66] Roth, Martha T. *Law Collections from Mesopotamia and Asia Minor.* 2nd ed. Atlanta, Ga.: Scholars Press, 1997.

HITTITES

Bryce, Trevor. *The Kingdom of the Hittites.* New York: Oxford University Press, 1998.

MacQueen, James G. *The Hittites and Their Contemporaries in Asia Minor.* Boulder, Colo.: Westview, 1975.

ISRAELITES

Bach, Alice. *Moses' Ark: Stories from the Bible.* New York, N.Y.: Delacorte Press, 1989.

Chaikin, Miriam. *Angels Sweep the Desert Floor: Bible Legends about Moses in the Wilderness.* New York: Clarion, 2002.

Coogan, Michael D., ed. *The Oxford History of the Biblical World.* New York: Oxford University Press, 1998.

Grant, Michael. *The History of Ancient Israel.* New York: Scribner, 1984.

Matthews, Victor H. *A Brief History of Ancient Israel.* Louisville, Ky.: Westminster John Knox Press, 2002.

Silberman, N. A. "Digging in the Land of the Bible." *Archaeology,* September/ October 1998.

Tubb, Jonathan N. *Bible Lands.* New York: Dorling Kindersley, 1991.

MYTHOLOGY

Black, Jeremy, and Anthony Green. *Gods, Demons, and Symbols of Ancient Mesopotamia: An Illustrated Dictionary.* London: British Museum Press, 1992.

[66] Bryson, Bernarda. *Gilgamesh: Man's First Story.* New York: Holt, Rinehart & Winston, 1967.

[66] Dalley, Stephanie. *Myths from Mesopotamia: Creation, the Flood, Gilgamesh, and Others.* New York: Oxford University Press, 1989.

Epic Heroes Issue. *Calliope,* January/February 1991.

Foster, Karen. *The City of Rainbows: A Tale from Ancient Sumer.* Philadelphia: University Museum, 1999.

[66] George, Andrew. *The Epic of Gilgamesh: A New Translation.* New York: Penguin, 1999.

McCaughrean, Geraldine. *Gilgamesh the Hero.* Grand Rapids, Mich.: Eerdmans, 2002.

[66] Sandars, Nancy K., ed. *Poems of Heaven and Hell from Ancient Mesopotamia.* Harmondsworth, U.K.: Penguin, 1971.

Zeman, Ludmila. *Gilgamesh the King.* Plattsburgh, N.Y.: Tundra Books, 1992.

———. *The Last Quest of Gilgamesh.* Plattsburgh, N.Y.: Tundra Books, 1995.

———. *The Revenge of Ishtar.* Plattsburgh, N.Y.: Tundra Books, 1993.

PERSIANS

Cook, John M. *The Persian Empire.* New York: Schocken, 1983.

[66] Herodotus. *The Histories.* Trans. Aubrey De Sélincourt. New York: Penguin, 1996.

SCIENCE

Moss, Carol. *Science in Ancient Mesopotamia.* New York: Franklin Watts, 1998.

SUMERIANS

Kramer, Samuel N. *History Begins at Sumer: Thirty-Nine "Firsts" in Recorded History.* Philadelphia: University of Pennsylvania Press, 1981.

———. *The Sumerians.* Chicago: University of Chicago Press, 1963.

Landau, Elaine. *The Sumerians.* Brookfield, Conn.: Millbrook Press, 1997.

Odjik, Pamela. *The Sumerians.* Englewood Cliffs, N.J.: Silver Burdett Press, 1990.

Sumer and Its City-States Issue. *Calliope,* September 2003.

WRITING

Swerdlow, J. L. "The Power of Writing." *National Geographic,* August 1999.

Walker, Christopher B. F. *Cuneiform.* Berkeley: University of California Press, 1987.

WEBSITES

All-in-One Biblical Resources Search
http://ntgateway.com/multibib/
Primary sources from the Bible, edited by Mark Goodacre, University of Birmingham, United Kingdom.

Ancient Art: Mesopotamia
http://www.dia.org/collections/ancient/mesopotamia/mesopotamia.html
A brief introduction from the Detroit Institute of Arts to the history and culture of ancient Mesopotamia, illustrated by objects from the museum's collection.

The Beginning of Writing and the First Alphabets
http://www.nb.no/baser/schoyen/4/4.4/441.html
Pictures of early Canaanite writing from Norway's Schoyen Collection.

Egypt's Golden Empire: Amenhotep III
http://www.pbs.org/empires/egypt/amenhotep.html
PBS website about Amenhotep III, with images of the king and some of the Amarna letters.

The Flood Narrative from the Gilgamesh Epic
http://pseudepigrapha.com/pseudepigrapha/gilgamesh.html
A translation by E. A. Speiser of the flood story in the Epic of Gilgamesh.

Hammurabi's Code of Laws
http://eawc.evansville.edu/anthology/hammurabi.htm
Hammurabi's code, translated by L. W. King. Part of a University of Evansville website called Exploring Ancient World Cultures.

Hattusha
http://www.hattuscha.de/eng/eng.html
A project of the German Institute of Archaeology, this website includes a history and photographic tour of the city of Hattusha, along with a time-line of excavations.

Internet Ancient History Sourcebook
http://www.fordham.edu/halsall/ancient/asbook.html
A website run by Fordham University of primary sources from the ancient world, including Mesopotamia, Egypt, Persia, and Israel. Includes such sources as the Legend of Sargon, Book of Exodus, and Sumerian proverbs.

The Johns Hopkins/University of Amsterdam Joint Expedition to Tell Umm el-Marra, Syria
http://www.jhu.edu/neareast/uem/index.html
Photos and findings from the Johns Hopkins/University of Amsterdam excavations at Umm el-Marra.

Mesopotamia
http://www.mesopotamia.co.uk/
A wealth of information about the ancient Near East, illustrated with objects from the collections of the British Museum. Topics include: Assyrian palaces and warfare; Babylonian astronomers; Mesopotamian geography, writing, and religion; royal tombs of Ur; trade and transport; and ziggurats.

Museum of the Ancient Near East in the Pergamon Museum
http://www.smb.spk-berlin.de/vam/e/s.html
Images of the Ishtar Gate in the Pergamon Museum in Berlin.

**The Northwest Palace of Ashur-nasir-pal II
at Nimrud**
*http://www.learningsites.com/NWPalace/
NWPalhome.html*
A virtual tour of the palace at Calhu (Nimrud).

The Oriental Institute
http://orientalinstitute.uchicago.edu/OI/default.html
Official website of the University of Chicago's
Oriental Institute, dedicated to documenting and
studying the languages, history and cultures of
the ancient Near East. Site includes: expedition
photographs from Persepolis; highlights of the
Institute's Canaan/Palestine and Mesopotamian
collections; objects stolen from the National
Museum in Baghdad in 2003; pictures of tells at
Babylon, Eridu, Calhu, Nineveh, Ur, and Uruk;
and virtual tours of the Institute's Mesopotamian
and Persian galleries.

Sumerian Inscription: Umma and Lagash
*http://www.northpark.edu/history/Classes/Sources/
UmmaLagash.html*
Documents found on clay cylinders that date
from about 2500 BCE. With explanatory notes
from the history department at North Park
University–Chicago.

INDEX

TEXT CREDITS

MAIN TEXT

p.24: James B. Pritchard, *Ancient Near Eastern Texts,* 3rd ed. with supplement (Princeton, N.J.: Princeton University Press, 1969), 615.

p.32: Sylvie Lackenbacher, "Un Texte vieux-babylonien sur la finition des textiles," *Syria* 59 (1982): 129–49.

p.36: Daniel Snell, trans. *Acta Sumerologica* 9 (1987) 239, number 12.

p.41: A. Leo Oppenheim, *Letters from Mesopotamia* (Chicago: University of Chicago Press, 1967), 94.

p.43: Benjamin Foster, *Before the Muses: An Anthology of Akkadian Literature,* vol. 2, 2nd ed. (Bethesda, Md: CDL Press, 1996), 533, 536.

p.45: Foster, *Before the Muses: An Anthology of Akkadian Literature,* vol. 2, 540–41, 556; vol. 1, 161–63.

p.52: Pritchard, *Ancient Near Eastern Texts,* 265; Jerrold S. Cooper, *Reconstructing History from Ancient Inscriptions: The Lagash-Umma Border Conflict* (Malibu, Calif.: Undena, 1983), 48.

pp. 55–56: Andrew George, trans. *The Epic of Gilgamesh: A New Translation* (New York: Penguin, 1999), 20, 44, 50, 61.

p.59: Foster, *Before the Muses: An Anthology of Akkadian Literature,* vol. 2, 803.

p.60: Pritchard, *Ancient Near Eastern Texts,* 267; Sabina Franke, "Kings of Akkad: Sargon and Naram-Sin," in *Civilizations of the Ancient Near East,* ed. Jack M. Sasson, et al. (New York: Scribner, 1995), 832.

p.61: Pritchard, *Ancient Near Eastern Texts,* 268.

p.63: Piotr Michalowski, *Letters from Early Mesopotamia.* Ed. Erica Reiner. Atlanta, Ga.: Scholars Press, 1993, 13–14.

p.64: Pritchard, *Ancient Near Eastern Texts,* 647–48.

p.66: Pritchard, *Ancient Near Eastern Texts,* 581.

p.68: W. Farber, "Witchcraft, Magic, and Divination in Ancient Mesopotamia," in *Civilizations of the Ancient Near East,* vol. 3, ed. Sasson et al., 1,908.

p.69: Pritchard, *Ancient Near Eastern Texts,* 597.

p.70: Pritchard, *Ancient Near Eastern Texts,* 585.

p.72: Martha Tobi Roth, *Law Collections from Mesopotamia and Asia Minor,* 2nd ed. (Atlanta, Ga.: Scholars Press, 1997), 16–17.

p.72: Roth, *Law Collections from Mesopotamia and Asia Minor,* 20; Postgate, *Early Mesopotamia: Society and Economy at the Dawn of History,* 84.

p.73: Roth, *Law Collections from Mesopotamia and Asia Minor,* 80.

p.74: Malcolm John Albert Horsnell, *The Year-Names of the First Dynasty of Babylon,* 2 vols. (Hamilton, Canada: McMaster University Press, 1999), 106.

p.75: Roth, *Law Collections from Mesopotamia and Asia Minor,* 121, 81.

p.77: Edward Chiera, *Old Babylonian Contracts* (Philadelphia: University Museum, 1922), 131–32.

p.78: Pritchard, *Ancient Near Eastern Texts,* 545.

p.79: Pritchard, *Ancient Near Eastern Texts,* 544–45.

p.81: Pritchard, *Ancient Near Eastern Texts,* 544–45.

p.82: Reuven Yaron, *The Laws of Eshnunna* (Jerusalem: Magnes Press, Hebrew University, 1969), 20–21.

p.83: Roth, *Law Collections from Mesopotamia and Asia Minor,* 101.

p.84: Roth, *Law Collections from Mesopotamia and Asia Minor,* 124.

p.87: Karel Van Lerberghe and Gabriella Voet, *Sippar-Amnanum, the Ur-Utu Archive,* vol. 1 (Winona Lake, Ind.: Eisenbrauns, 1991), 31.

p.88: Roth, *Law Collections from Mesopotamia and Asia Minor,* 105; Raymond Westbrook, *Old Babylonian Marriage Law* (Horn, Austria: Ferdinand Berger und Sohne, 1988), 119.

p.89: Oppenheim, *Letters from Mesopotamia,* 86.

p.91: Samuel Noah Kramer, *The Sumerians* (Chicago: University of Chicago Press, 1963), 237–40.

p.94: Kramer, *The Sumerians,* 241–42; Amanda H. Podany, *The Land of Hana: Kings, Chronology and Scribal Tradition* (Bethesda, Md.: CDL Press, 2002), 119; Kramer, *The Sumerians,* 236.

p.95: Bertrand Lafont, "The Women of the Palace of Mari" in *Everyday Life in Ancient Mesopotamia,* ed. Jean Bottero (Baltimore, Md: Johns Hopkins University Press, 2001), 127–140.

p.97: Jack M. Sasson, "Biographical Notices on Some Royal Ladies from Mari," *Journal of Cuneiform Studies* 25 (1973): 65.

p.98: Sasson, "Biographical Notices on Some Royal Ladies from Mari"; Lafont, "The Women of the Palace of Mari," 133.

p.101: Albert Kirk Grayson, *Assyrian and Babylonian Chronicles* (Locust Valley, N.Y.: J. J. Augustin, 1975), 156.

p.102: Trevor Bryce, *Kingdom of the Hittites* (Oxford: Clarendon, 1998), 103.

p.103: Bryce, *Kingdom of the Hittites,* 84.

p.107: William L. Moran, *The Amarna Letters* (Baltimore, Md.: Johns Hopkins University Press, 1992), 57.

p.109: Moran, *The Amarna Letters,* 1.

p.112: Bryce, *Kingdom of the Hittites,* 368, 367.

p.114: Pritchard, *Ancient Near Eastern Texts,* 653–54.

p.117: I Samuel 9:2, 17:8b-9, 17:48-50.

p.119: I Kings 16:16; Pritchard, *Ancient Near Eastern Texts,* 320.

p.120: Genesis 1:1-5.

p.121: Genesis 6:13, 6: 14, 7:16b-17; Foster, *Before the Muses: An Anthology of Akkadian Literature,* vol. 1, 181.

p.123: Genesis 11:6.

p.124: Genesis 12:1–2; 39:2, 4; 45:1–3.

p.125: II Kings 22:8.

p.126: II Kings 22:13.

pp.126–127: Exodus 1:16, 2:3, 5:1, 10:15, 10:28.

p.128: Deuteronomy 5: 7–21.

p.134: Daniel David Luckenbill, *Ancient Records of Assyria and Babylonia,* vol. 1 (Chicago: University of Chicago Press, 1926), 144–45.

p.135: Pritchard, *Ancient Near Eastern Texts,* 560.

p.136: Luckenbill, *Ancient Records of Assyria and Babylonia,* 143, 211; II Kings 17: 5-6.

p.138: Luckenbill, *Ancient Records of Assyria and Babylonia,* vol. 2, 339–41.

p.139: Amélie Kuhrt, *The Ancient Near East,* vol. 2 (New York: Routledge, 1995), 613.

p.141: After a translation by A. K. Grayson, Assyrian and Babylonian Chronicles (1975), no. 5: 11-13; quoted in Kuhrt, *The Ancient Near East,* vol. 2, 591; II Kings 24: 10-12, 24:14, 25:1, 25:3-4.

p.142: Pritchard, *Ancient Near Eastern Texts,* 308.

p.143: Herodotus, *The Histories,* trans. Aubrey de Selincourt (New York: Penguin, 1972), 113; Psalm 137: 1-2, 4.

p.145: Tremper Longman, trans., *Fictional Akkadian Autobiography* (Winona Lake, Ind.: Eisenbrauns, 1991), 225–28.

p.146: Longman, *Fictional Akkadian Autobiography* 225–28.

p.147: Pritchard, *Ancient Near Eastern Texts,* 562.

p.148: Pritchard, *Ancient Near Eastern Texts,* 334.

p.149: Pritchard, *Ancient Near Eastern Texts,*
315–16.

p.150: Herodotus, *The Histories,* 75.

p.152: Pritchard, *Ancient Near Eastern Texts,*
315–16; Isaiah 44: 24, 28.

pp. 158–59: Wilfred G. Lambert, *Babylonian
Wisdom Literature* (Oxford: Oxford University
Press, 1960), 239–50, 260–62.

SIDEBARS

p.44: Foster, *Before the Muses,* 181.

p.73: Malcolm John Albert Horsnell, *The Year-
Names of the First Dynasty of Babylon,* 2 vols.
(Hamilton, Canada: McMaster University Press,
1999), 106.

p.100: Jean Bottero, "The Oldest Cuisine in the
World," in *Everyday Life in Ancient Mesopotamia,*
trans. Antonia Nevill (Baltimore, Md.: Johns
Hopkins University Press, 2001), 57.

p.118: Pritchard, *Ancient Near Eastern Texts,* 422.

p.131: Psalm 119: 33–34, 73.

PICTURE CREDITS

ACKNOWLEDGMENTS

We would like to thank our wonderful editors and friends, Karen Fein, Nancy Toff, and Ron Mellor for their invaluable help with this book. We are also grateful to Brigit Dermott for copyediting, Amy Henderson who laid out the book, Glenn Schwartz and Bill Propp for their interviews, Mary Kay Linge for coordinating the maps, Christine Buese and Justine Bertucelli for picture research, Diane Brooks and Dan Fleming for their careful reading of the manuscript, Tammi Schneider and Martha Roth for their suggestions about the initial proposal, Marc Van De Mieroop for his excellent comments, and Daniel Snell for his translation of the messenger tablet. Hundreds of schoolchildren—our very special test pilots—teachers, and librarians read the manuscript and offered valuable, lively critique. To each one, we offer sincere appreciation. Finally, we are grateful for the contributions of family members: to Emily Podany for finding a passage in *Lord of the Rings* for the Gilgamesh chapter and to Jerry Podany and Sears McGee for innumerable excellent suggestions.

MARNI MCGEE was born in New Orleans and grew up in Charlotte, North Carolina. Her love of words began in childhood. She remembers sitting around the dinner table at night with her father, mother, older sister, and younger brother— all talking about the day. Along with the fried chicken and grits were dishes of laughter, teasing, memories, and stories. Many of her books spring from these family experiences. She began writing children's books in 1974 and has been a full-time writer since 1994. Her work—published in the United States, United Kingdom, and Korea— includes award-winning picture books, easy readers, poetry, and historical fiction. She is an avid traveler with a special love for England and Italy. Her "favorite things" include beach walks, reading, theater, and music, especially chamber music and opera. McGee lives with her husband in Santa Barbara, California, and is the mother of two grown children.

RONALD MELLOR, who is professor of history at UCLA, first became enthralled with ancient history as a student at Regis High School in New York City. He is the statewide faculty advisor of the California History–Social Science Project (CHSSP), which brings university faculty together with K-12 teachers at sites throughout California. In 2000, the American Historical Association awarded the CHSSP the Albert J. Beveridge Award for K-12 teaching. Professor Mellor has held fellowships from the National Endowment for the Humanities and the American Council of Learned Societies. His research has centered on ancient religion and Roman historiography. His books include *Theia Rhome: The Goddess Roma in the Greek World* (1975), *From Augustus to Nero: The First Dynasty of Imperial Rome* (1990), *Tacitus* (1993), *Tacitus: The Classical Heritage* (1995), *The Historians of Ancient Rome* (1997), and *The Roman Historians* (2nd edition, 2004).

AMANDA PODANY is a specialist in the history of the ancient Near East and a professor of history at California State Polytechnic University, Pomona. She has taught there since 1990 and is currently serving as the director of the university's honors program. From 1993 to 1997 she was executive director of the California History–Social Science Project, a professional development program for history–social science teachers at all grade levels. Her work in professional development for teachers has received major grants from the California Postsecondary Education Commission and the United States Department of Education. Her publications include *The Land of Hana: Kings, Chronology, and Scribal Tradition*. Professor Podany has also published numerous journal articles on ancient Near Eastern history and on approaches to teaching. She lives in Los Angeles with her husband and two children.